D1790113

STUDENT WORKBOOK

BEGINNING CURRICULA A, B AND AFFIXES USED IN SIGNING EXACT ENGLISH

Modern Signs Press, Inc.

INDEX

PREFACE

This workbook is meant for use in a class supplemented with material from the book <u>Teaching and Learning Signing Exact English</u>, (Modern Signs Press, 1983), and/or with the video-tapes available illustrating the lessons in Curriculum A and B.

The student should also read the introductory pages to the <u>Signing Exact English</u> text for the background information on the rationale and philosophy of this sytem.

Included in this workbook is an explanation of the Sign Continuum, a list and discussion of What's Important, and the Signing Exact English principles for basic, complex and compound words with worksheets.

The student should particularly note the section on Adding Principles from American Sign Language to Signing Exact English.

I. THE SIGN LANGUAGE CONTINUUM

What is it?

In the United States, there is a great variety in signs
used. These signs range along a continuum from nonverbal
communication through American Sign Language to manual
representations of English. The chart on page 24
depicts this continuum. Expert signers may shift from
place to place on the continuum depending on the
situation, the person(s) being addressed, and the topic
as well as on their own repertiore of skills.

In-Group Signs refers to those signs which are understood only by a limited group. Within this category,
Home Signs refers to signs which are used within a
family, and not understood outside the family. These
are usually relatively few signs, whether used by deaf
families for a few words or concepts, or by hearing
families who have not been exposed to standardized
signs. One example would be the drawing of the arches
in the air when referring to McDonald's.

School Signs refer to signs developed and used by the
children within a school. The extent of these signs
may depend on the children's exposure to adult models.
In extreme cases there may be extensive use of such
signs, which are not understood outside of the school
population. Examples would be tapping the nose with
the middle finger for DOG (wet nose), tapping the
bridge of the nose twice for WOMAN (probably from
speech lessons on the nasalized M and N sounds), etc.

Local Signs are regional usages among deaf adults.
Just as in spoken English most words are common, but
there are regional variations as in what a one-room
apartment is called (studio? efficiency? bachelor?),
there are variations in signs depending on what part
of the country one is from. One example is the
various signs for FOOTBALL.

AMERICAN SIGN LANGUAGE, AMESLAN, or ASL

American Sign Language, Ameslan, or ASL has come in
for an increasing amount of study in recent years
aimed at analyzing the rules of grammar that exist
in this language. Research is turning up definite
grammatical principles that are often completely un-
related to the grammatical rules of English--such as
reduplication (of nouns to show plurality, of verbs
to show continuing or habitual action), directionality

(continued)

(to indicate the subject-verb-object relationship, for instance), and word order (e.g. chronological order or the placing of the most striking feature first). ASL, like any other language, has its own vocabulary, idioms, and grammar, and is as different from English as any foreign language.

SIGN ENGLISH, PIDGIN SIGN ENGLISH (PSE), CONCEPTUALLY ACCURATE SIGNED ENGLISH (CASE)

The traditional signs of Ameslan are used, but in simultaneous communication which is based on English, the signs are sorted out according to English word order. This becomes a sort of pidgin language, taking its vocabulary from Ameslan and its structure from English. Because of the differences between the two languages, signs, even when sorted out in English word order, do not completely represent English words; also, there are English words for which there are no Ameslan signs, and Ameslan idioms which are difficult to translate into English. Few, if any, endings (-ing, -s, -ed, etc.) are used in Sign English.

MANUAL ENGLISH

There are several sign systems under this heading, and the basic rationale for their development stemmed from dissatisfaction with the poor educational showing of many deaf children, the need for input before output can be expected, and the lack of ease and clarity in the presentation of English through other existing visual modes (lipreading, listening, reading, etc.). Sign English, as noted above, does not present a clear, grammatically complete version of English. Accordingly, in varying degrees, new sign systems attempt to provide manual signs to supplement already existing signs and increase the input to the child of both vocabulary and English markers, word endings, pronouns and other structural elements. All systems use (1) word endings, affixes, verb tenses; (2) the creation of signs for English words previously having no signs; (3) the use of initials with base signs to create sign families for words similar in meaning and sharing a common traditional sign.

(continued)

FINGERSPELLING

Fingerspelling is the most accurate rendition of English in manual form. The Rochester Method and Visual English use fingerspelling in combination with speech. It is not easy to spell at a normal speaking rate, but fingerspelling is an important component of Total Communication.

NOTE:

Although word-for-word translation of ASL makes it look like bad English, it must be stressed that this is no more the case than word-for-word translation of French, Russian, or Chinese would be bad English.

Examples: ASL--School finish, zoom me.
Sign English--When school close, I am leave fast.
Manual English--When school closes, I am leaving fast.

The decision about what type of signs to use depends on the purpose of the communication and the audience, and right and wrong are situationally defined.

NON-VERBAL COMMUNICATION	IN-GROUP SIGNS			AMERICAN SIGN LANGUAGE	SIGN ENGLISH	MANUAL ENGLISH	FINGERSPELLING
	HOME SIGNS	SCHOOL SIGNS	LOCAL SIGNS				
Pantomime Natural gestures Facial expressions Body movement				Standard signs, some finger-spelling elements of pantomime, syntax of its own.	Standard signs, fingerspelling, a lot of English syntax, little or no use of endings.	Standard signs supplemented with invented signs to show English inflections, affixes, new vocabulary.	Letter by letter representation of English
				Sign by meaning	Sign by meaning.	Some sign by English word, some by meaning, depending on system.	
	Childrenese			ASL Ameslan	Signed English Manual English Pidgin Sign English PSE CASE (Conceptually Accurate Signed English) Ameslish Siglish	Seeing Essential English (SEE 1) Signing Exact English (SEE 2) Linguistics of Visual English (LOVE) Signed English Manual English	Rochester method Visible English

Manually Coded English (MCE) is a label covering Sign English, Manual English, and Fingerspelling.

4

II. WHAT'S IMPORTANT?

<u>Some very important questions.</u> . .

1. Can a person include all the signs, endings, etc.?
2. Doesn't it slow you down?
3. Does it really help kids develop better English?

The answer to all the above is . . . yes.

Many people do not sign everything they say. This is not new. It was one reason why one of the original ten tenets was that input must precede output, since the child cannot give back language which he never received. We must be aware of what we are signing, and why we are signing that way. In 1973, in a survey of programs for the deaf, Donald Moores reported that

. . . most teachers in combined programs did not consistently use sign/spelled English in coordination with the spoken word. The signed or spelled element frequently represented key words and not full sentences.

This is related to the second question. Especially for persons who are not yet fluent in signs, it does slow a person down to sign every word, and every ending. It becomes, then, a question of priority. If we are interested in maintaining normal speaking speed, even for beginning signers, it is likely some signs will be dropped. We cannot then, however, be surprised when the children do not develop the usage of those words or parts of words which were dropped. This should be a conscious decision at some point, not the path of least resistance.

When consistent use of a manual English system at home and in school is observed, children are appearing with excellent English skills.

<u>Some important factors.</u> . .

1. <u>Attitudes and expectations.</u>

    Positive attitudes are of prime importance. Children will live up to, or down to, the expectations we have of them. Studies of the self-fulfilling prophecy are well known. Studies of inner-city schools have indicated that one of the chief factors in the success of children is the positive attitude and expectations of their teachers. This does not, of course, mean setting up unreasonable

5

demands on the child, but in too many cases children are limited more by the low expectations of those around them than by their own disability.

2. Organization of program or curriculum.

Studies in general education are indicating that when a program follows an organized curriculum, it is more successful than a program that does not. It seems to matter less what the specific curriculum is than the fact that it is organized. A hit-or-miss, free-for-all approach in teaching often does not reach its goal because it has neither a clear goal nor a clear program for getting there.

3. Parents . . . especially mothers.

The mother has the most contact with the child during the early formative years. It has been reported by studies of Army inductees that the educational level of the mother has the most influence on the achievement level of the child. Crandall (1975) reported that when mothers of preschoolers used endings, the child developed such usage, and there was more influence from the mother's usage than from what was used in the school.

4. The early years.

Studies of hearing children's language development, and studies now beginning to appear on the development of American Sign Language in deaf children of deaf parents, emphasize the importance of the first few years of life in the language learning process. The fact that a child has missed an early start is not necessarily disastrous, however; some children and their families have begun Total Communication at six years of age and progressed very well.

5. Consistency and follow-through.

This is much the same as an organized program. While variation in signs is natural and children are more flexible than adults, it is not helpful for every person in the child's environment to use a different sign for the same word.

6. Skill development.

   While positive attitudes are of prime importance, easy communication means that parents and teachers need to improve their skills as time goes by. Parents of young babies can grow in skill along with their children, and fathers usually have less time to devote to the learning of this skill than mothers do. Teachers are not in the same situation as parents, and should acquire fluency for effectiveness.

7. Awareness of what we are doing.

   This is very important. As mentioned above, individuals often do not sign everything they say. Usually this is quite unconscious. We think we are signing English because we are speaking English at the same time as we sign. In cases of sign selection, also, we need to know why we are choosing a specific sign over others.

8. ALWAYS signing in the deaf child's presence.

   This is a cardinal rule. The impact of signing, or not signing, is felt not only on the language input but on the psychological effect. Not signing implies that the child is not important, that he or she has no right to know what is being said in his or her presence. If we would not say something in front of a hearing child, we should not say it in front of a deaf child taking advantage of the fact that he cannot hear us. This is not simply bad manners, it is a blow against the child's self-concept. Similarly, even when the conversation does not relate to the child, the possibility of incidental language input is important. A deaf child is never going to overhear as much language as a hearing child does, and all language input is important.

Communication alone is not enough.

While communication is the heart and soul of programs for the deaf, it is not the only important element. Skill in signing is not enough. If this would resolve all problems, all hearing children with hearing teachers would have good teachers and good education programs. . . and this is not the case. We also need to give deaf children knowledge of various subject areas, a strong self-concept and self-confidence, and the ability to deal with the world as a deaf person.

What are nonsigning aids to communication?

Try repeating . . . rephrasing . . . saying it differently. Use examples. Use visuals . . . overhead transparencies, pictures, charts, objects . . . or real experiences. Be aware of visibility . . . is the light good enough? Is the light behind you or on your face? What is the background (striped wallpaper, striped shirts, and the like are murder on the eyes)? Are the signs, print, pictures of a size that can be easily seen? How about skits, role playing, dramatizations? How about choral repetition, songs, games that teach? Labelling things? Making charts of common requests, of basic sentences? Let's try riddles for thinking skills . . . asking what doesn't belong . . . working with opposites, analogies, following directions, retelling stories, doing interviews.

III. MANUAL ENGLISH AND SIGNING EXACT ENGLISH RULES

A. Manual English systems generally have <u>three types of additions</u>:

1. word endings, tenses, affixes: -ing, -ness, -ment, un-, etc.

   The fewest such markers are used by the Gallaudet Preschool Signed English system, aimed at pre-schoolders, which uses only about 12.

   The most are used by Seeing Essential English.

2. New signs for English words previously having no single sign, e.g.:

   fruit (in ASL, apple-orange-banana-etc.)
   vegetable
   parent (in ASL, mother-father)
   toy
     etc.

   The Signed English series uses ASL word compounds, such as hair-yellow for blond. Signing Exact English uses ASL signs when they are not such compounds and when they normally translate to only one English equivalent, e.g. "can't", "careless", etc.

3. Use of initials with base signs

   class: family, group, team, etc.
    make: produce, create
   friend: acquaint, mate, neighbor, relate

   All Manual English systems sign the structural components of English: articles, auxiliaries, pronouns, affixes, etc. to enable deaf children to develop a grasp of the syntax and patterns of English, not merely its vocabulary. This grasp of syntax and patterns is perhaps the most crucial factor in developing mastery of English.

B. The basic rules of <u>Signing Exact English</u> .

1. Words are considered in <u>three groups</u>: basic, compound, and complex.

   A. A Basic word is considered to be one in which no more can be taken away and still have a word remaining, e.g.: girl, run, happy.

The basic rules of Signing Exact English, (continued)

      B.   A Complex word is a basic word plus an affix or tense marker, e.g.: girls, running, unhappy.

      C.   A Compound word is two basic words used together, blackbird, babysit.

2.   For basic words, the two out of three rule is followed:

             spelling, sound, meaning

If any two are the same, the word is signed the same (see No. 5 below).

Example:

Right, rite, write are all signed differently because only sound is the same.

To wind a watch and to hear the wind are signed differently because only spelling is the same.

To bear a child, to bear with me, to meet a bear are all signed the same because spelling and sound are the same.

To live in California and to catch a live fish are signed the same because the spelling and the basic meaning are the same.

3.   For complex words, the affix is added in signs if it is added in speech or writing. It is not dependent on the work class . . . e.g. -ing is used for adjectives, verbs, nouns, etc.; -s is used for plurals and third person singular of verbs:

girls, talks, running, interesting, morning, unhappy

4.   For compound words, the word is signed as the component basic words if, and only if, the meaning is derived from or related to the meanings of the component words; e.g. cowbow and undercook would be signed cow-boy and under-cook, but since the meaning of understand is not related to either under cr stand, it would be signed understand, as a basic word. Similarly, forget would have one basic sign, not for-get.

5.   If an inflection, such as past tense, is added to a basic word, the resulting word is not a basic word. Accordingly, saw would not follow the two out of three rule in "I saw you yesterday" and "I bought a new saw." The first would be signed as see plus past tense; the second as the basic word saw. The same is true of "I left town yesterday" and "turn left".

Examples of basic, multiple meaning words.

I told Roz that after I finished running off some copies, I was going to run off with her husband. She told me if I would stop running off at the mouth so much, she might believe me more. We almost had a run in about it, but then she noticed she had a run in her stocking and ran off to change. While she was gone I ran into Tom and he told me there would be a run off election for the president of his class. He was really excited and ran on and on about it. I finally had to leave as I was running late with my schedule for the day and I had to run down several people before I could leave. Anyway, Tom was starting to run down his opponent, and I didn't like that. I had no trouble getting my car started--it runs fine since the tuneup--but then I ran into trouble with the runoffs from yesterday's rain. Would you believe that by the time the other cars got through a flooded area I had run out of gas? Then I was in such a hurry to get to a meeting that I ran a red light and got caught. I'm really worried about running up a lot of tickets and getting a bad driving record. When I finally got to the meeting, the guy who was running it gave me a bad time for being late. I really was mad, and told him I had almost run into a tree in my hurry to get there, and did run over some broken glass, and with such a run of bad luck he was lucky to see me there at all. By the time I got home I was cold and miserable, and woke up this morning with a runny nose. My eyes are running, too. To top it all off, I threw my clothes in the washer last night without looking closely, and the colors ran. Is it any wonder that when I ran up the flag this morning, it was upside down?

11

Examples of basic, multiple meaning words, cont'd

John is <u>running</u>.
The water is <u>running</u>.
Your nose is <u>running</u>.
The motor is <u>running</u>.
That man is <u>running</u> for the bus.
That man is <u>running</u> for mayor.
My eyes are <u>running</u>.
The bus <u>runs</u> between Chicago and New York.
His tongue <u>ran</u> on and on.
Thoughts <u>ran</u> in his head.
Her stocking has a <u>run</u>.
He hit a home <u>run</u>.
The butter is <u>running</u>.
Days <u>ran</u> into weeks.
I <u>ran</u> into a friend.
I <u>ran</u> into a tree.
The play <u>ran</u> for a year.
I <u>ran</u> into trouble.
Use a <u>running</u> stitch.
Who is <u>running</u> the store?
<u>Run</u> an ad in the paper.
It will be OK in the long <u>run</u>.
You look <u>run</u> down.
To <u>run</u> someone down.
We <u>ran</u> out of money.
Someone <u>ran</u> over my dog.
<u>Run</u> up the flag.
<u>Run</u> off some copies.
etc.
etc.
etc.

Draw a <u>right</u> angle.
Your behavior was <u>right</u>.
Your answer was <u>right</u>.
It's on your <u>right</u> side.
He leans to the <u>right</u> in his politics.
It's your <u>right</u> to say what you think.
Go <u>right</u> home.
I want it <u>right</u> now.
The cold went <u>right</u> through me.
I'll meet you <u>right</u> here.
They <u>righted</u> the boat.
The maid <u>righted</u> the room.
She put it to <u>rights</u>.
Go to the office <u>right</u> away.
Who has the <u>right</u> of way?

IV. WORKSHEET ON BASIC, COMPOUND, COMPLEX WORDS

Basic words are words that do not have affixes added to them. S.E.E. II uses a three point criteria to determine the sign used for a basic word. The principle is--if any two of the following are the same then the same sign would be used:

      1. spelling
      2. sound
      3. meaning

NOTE: If an inflection such as past tense is added, a word is not considered a basic word.

Example:

I left my saw at home.   spelling: *different*   sign: *different*
He saw a blue bird.   sound: *same*
                    meaning: *different*

      In the first sentence "saw" is a basic word, but in the second sentence "saw" is the past tense of "see". The two are not signed the same.

(Note: answer key is in Teaching and Learning Signing Exact English.)

Use the three point criteria to determine how the underlined words in each sentence would be signed.

1. I had a ball at the party.   spelling: *same*   sign: *same*
                         sound: *same*
2. Mom, buy me a new ball.   meaning: *different*

3. Turn left at the corner.   spelling: *(past tense*   sign: *different*
4. I left my purse in the car.   sound: *of "leave")*
                         meaning: *different*

5. I like new clothes.   spelling: sign:
6. You look like your brother.   sound:
                         meaning:

7. We might go to church.   spelling: sign:
8. I tried with all my might to move the refrigerator.   sound:
                         meaning:

9. I wear plain clothes.   spelling: sign:
10. She made the directions plain.   sound:
                         meaning:

11. I'll plant the seeds.   spelling: sign:
12. This plant is dead.   sound:
                         meaning:

IV. Worksheet on Basic, Compound, Complex words, cont'd

13. Thanks for the birthday   spelling: sign:
    present.   sound:
14. The lawyer will present   meaning:
    his argument.

15. Would you like to store   spelling: sign:
    your furniture in my   sound:
    garage?   meaning:
16. I'll buy some fruit at
    the store.

17. Call me at the office.   spelling: sign:
18. The teacher will call   sound:
    on him.   meaning:
19. The doctor is on call.

20. That was a close call.   spelling: sign:
21. Please close the door.   sound:
                                 meaning:

22. We're having company for   spelling: sign:
    dinner.   sound:
23. His company went out of   meaning:
    business.

24. My glass is full.   spelling: sign:
25. Fill your plate with food.   sound:
                                 meaning:

26. The road is only 12 feet   spelling: sign:
    wide.   sound:
27. My feet hurt.   meaning:

28. Can you see without your   spelling: sign:
    glasses?   sound:
29. They would make good   meaning:
    drinking glasses.

30. She received two letters.   spelling: sign:
31. Do you know the letters   sound:
    of the alphabet?   meaning:

32. Line up, please.   spelling: sign:
33. Don't feed me any line.   sound:
34. He lost his fishing line.   meaning:

35. Please turn the light on.   spelling: sign:
36. It's still light outside.   sound:
37. I like light colored cars.   meaning:

14

IV. Worksheet on basic, compound, complex words, cont'd

38. What do you <u>mean</u>?   spelling: sign:
39. She's <u>mean</u> to her sister.   sound:
                          meaning:

40. Take all the <u>objects</u> off   spelling: sign:
    the desk.   sound:
41. He <u>objects</u> to closing the   meaning:
    college.

42. What <u>kind</u> of bread is   spelling: sign:
    this?   sound:
43. Thanks for being so <u>kind</u>. meaning:

Would the sign for the underlined word in each of
the two phrases be signed the same way or differently?

		<u>Same</u>	<u>Different</u>
1.	She <u>left</u> home. Please turn <u>left</u>.	____	____
2.	The <u>wind</u> is blowing. It's time to <u>wind</u> the clock.	____	____
3.	The answer is the empty <u>set</u>. Did you <u>set</u> the date?	____	____
4.	The <u>late</u> John Smith. Are you <u>late</u>?	____	____
5.	<u>Saw</u> the wood. I <u>saw</u> him.	____	____
6.	<u>Dry</u> the dishes. His sense of humor is <u>dry</u>.	____	____
7.	Give me a cough <u>drop</u>. <u>Drop</u> your hands.	____	____
8.	<u>Park</u> the car Let's go to the <u>park</u>.	____	____
9.	The <u>will</u> was left by my late aunt. <u>Will</u> you go with me?	____	____
10.	The <u>mine</u> was deep. It is <u>mine</u>.	____	____

IV. Worksheet on basic, compound, complex words, cont'd

1. Some of the following words are compound, some are complex and some are basic words. Break the words down according to how they would be signed.

2. Remember a compound word is signed as two basic words only if the two basic words do not distort the meaning of the compound word. For example, the compound word butterfly has one sign because to sign butter + fly would not be consistent with the meaning of the compound word.

sang = *sing* + *-ed*

along = *along*

mailman = *mail + man*

understand =

always =

forget =

misbehave =

impossible =

beautiful =

babysit =

sat =

busy =

gravy -

lucky =

because =

beyond =

wives =

stories =

series =

religious =

serious =

secret =

secretary =

limitation =

injury =

behind =

handsome =

dependence =

independence =

weight =

diet =

chalkboard =

vocation =

already =

doubtful =

chemistry =

yardstick =

wristwatch =

wisdom =

worker =

shower =

mastermind =

sign =

resign =

comfortable =

disagree =

chatter =

different =

disappointed =

handmade =

Worksheet on basic, compound, complex words, cont'd

sentence =   candle =

sent =   busy =

fruitflies =   broken =

cracker =   breakfast =

present =

represent =

governor =

Write the word which these basic words plus a prefix, suffix, or marker, make.

1. "exam" + "tion"   _____

2. "see" + "ed"   _____

3. "happy" + "ly"   _____

4. "Egypt" + "an"   _____

5. "sign" + "ure"   _____

6. "enthuse" + "ic"   _____

7. "China" + "ese"   _____

8. "vary" + "ous"   _____

9. "simple" + "ity"   _____

10. "intellect" + "ence" _____

11. "sink" + "en"   _____

12. "occupy" + "ant"   _____

13. "female" + "ine"   _____

14. "specific" + "ify"   _____

15. "critic" + "ize"   _____

V. ADDING PRINCIPLES FROM AMERICAN SIGN LANGUAGE TO SIGNING EXACT ENGLISH

Some features that appear in American Sign Language can and should be used with Signing Exact English to add clarity and expressiveness. These include facial expressions and body movements related to negatives, questions, pronouns, plurals, and other such grammatical elements.

For instance, when asking a question that can be answered with yes or no (Do you want some candy?), the eyebrows should be raised, while when asking a question using WH words (what, why, when, where, who, how) it is common to frown slightly. Try this when signing the questions, beginning with Lesson 1.

With negatives, clarity is aided if a headshake is included when signing the negative (no, not, isn't, don't, etc.). This should be included with Lesson 2, for instance.

When signing a demonstrative pronoun (this, that, these, those) you should note that for this and these, the object is usually near the speaker, while for that and those it is further away. Point the hand towards the location involved in the statement. If they are not present, use your imagination to establish them in locations. When using personal pronouns (he, him, she, her, etc.) you should make the sign toward the person referred to, or make the sign and then point (with either hand). When the person is not present, use an imaginary location. If more than one person is referred to in the sentence, set them up in different locations (e.g. one on your right, one on your left).

Plurals can be clarified by making the sign twice before adding the -s. For instance, the sign for <u>girl</u> should be made only once for one girl, but twice with an -s added after the second for <u>girls</u>. For some signs this indication of plurals may be more easily done by moving the sign slightly to the side before adding the -s, as in <u>trees</u>.

In American Sign Language, some signs for verbs can change direction to move towards the object of the verb. For instance, <u>give</u> may be signed from the giver towards the receiver.

Use your eyes . . . look up when talking about things above you (such as the ceiling) and make your signs somewhat higher; look down when speaking of things below you. Use your face . . . smile when speaking of happy things, look sad when speaking of sad things. Use the size of your signs . . . or the speed . . . larger signs can emphasize greater size or intensity, while a slow sign can illustrate the slowness with which something was done ("he walked slowly").

These facial expressions and body movements do a great deal to reflect "tone of voice" and add color as well as meaning to signed English.

BEGINNING CURRICULUM A SIGNING EXACT ENGLISH

Modern Signs Press, Inc.

This section of the student workbook for Beginning Curriculum A of Signing Exact English includes vocabulary lists and practice sentences for the fourteen lessons which contain approximately 750 words and affixes.

Be verbs, pronouns, introductions

1.	am	26.	how
2.	are	27.	meet
3.	is	28.	morning
4.	I	29.	name
5.	you	30.	nice
6.	he	31.	night
7.	she	32.	no
8.	it	33.	please
9.	we	34.	sorry
10.	they	35.	stop
11.	my	36.	thank
12.	your	37.	that
13.	his	38.	time
14.	her	39.	to
15.	our	40.	town
16.	their	41.	up
17.	afternoon	42.	welcome
18.	bed	43.	what
19.	evening	44.	where
20.	fine	45.	yes
21.	get	46.	-ing
22.	go, come	47.	-s
23.	good	48.	'm
24.	happy	49.	're
25.	home	50.	's

Practice Sentences

1. Good morning!
2. Good afternoon!
3. Good evening!
4. Good night!
5. It's time to get up. It is time to get up.
6. It's time to go to bed. It is time to go to bed.
7. I'm going to bed. Am I going to bed?
8. Is she going to bed? She's going to bed.
9. Is he going to bed? He's going to bed.
10. You're going to bed. Where are you going?
11. Where are we going? We're going to town.
12. Where are they going? They're going home.
13. How are you?
14. I'm fine!
15. Thanks!
16. Thank you!
17. You're welcome!
18. Please go to bed.
19. No!
20. Stop that!
21. I'm sorry.
22. Yes, that's fine.
23. What's your name?
24. Where is his home?
25. I'm happy to meet you.
26. Welcome to our town.
27. Please go get her.
28. That's my bed.
29. He's coming to my home.
30. Where is she?

CURRICULUM A, LESSON 2

Lesson 2. Fruits, dishes, drinks, family

1.	a, an	26.	knife
2.	and	27.	lemon
3.	all right	28.	lime
4.	apple	29.	milk
5.	apricot	30.	mother
6.	banana	31.	napkin
7.	berry	32.	not
8.	bowl	33.	of
9.	brother	34.	orange
10.	chair	35.	pan
11.	cherry	36.	peach
12.	coffee	37.	pear
13.	cup	38.	pineapple
14.	date	39.	plate
15.	desk	40.	plum
16.	dish	41.	pot
17.	door	42.	sister
18.	father	43.	spoon
19.	fig	44.	tea
20.	fruit	45.	these
21.	fork	46.	this
22.	glass	47.	those
23.	grape	48.	water
24.	grapefruit	49.	window
25.	juice	50.	-ne, -en

Practice Sentences

1. That's my plate.

2. That's all right. That is all right.

3. That's O.K. That is O.K.

4. What's this? What is this?

5. This is an apple.

6. This is a table.

7. This is a ball.

8. This is not a chair.

9. This is a window.

10. This is a bowl of fruit.

11. This is not a desk.

12. What's that? What is that?

13. That is a pot of tea.

14. That is a fig.

15. That is a date.

16. That is not a spoon.

17. That is a knife.

18. That is a fork.

19. That is a dish of cherries.

20. That is a grapefruit.

21. What are those?

22. Those are chairs.

23. Those are bananas.

24. Those are grapes.

25. Those are peaches.

26. Those are lemons.

27. Those are pears.

28. Those are limes.

29. Those are oranges.

30. What are these?

31. These are pots and pans.

32. These are cups.

33. These are glasses of pineapple juice.

34. This is a plate of plums.

35. This is a cup of coffee.

36. That is a glass of milk.

37. That is a glass of water.

38. Where is your mother?

39. What is your sister's name?

40. How is your father?

41. Where's her brother?

42. Please get a napkin.

43. That's your chair, not mine.

44. He's gone home.

45. That's mine!

Lesson 3. Past tense, vegetables, snacks, meals

1.	bean	26.	more
2.	bread	27.	much
3.	breakfast	28.	on
4.	cabbage	29.	onion
5.	cake	30.	pea
6.	candy	31.	pie
7.	carrot	32.	potato
8.	celery	33.	put
9.	cereal	34.	radish
10.	cookie	35.	salad
11.	corn	36.	see
12.	cucumber	37.	snack
13.	dinner	38.	some
14.	do	39.	spinach
15.	drink	40.	squash
16.	eat	41.	supper
17.	egg	42.	the
18.	fish	43.	toast
19.	for	44.	tomato
20.	ice cream	45.	vegetable
21.	lettuce	46.	very
22.	like	47.	want
23.	lunch	48.	-ed, past tense
24.	many	49.	n't
25.	meat		

Practice Sentences

1. Did you see his mother?

2. Do you want a banana?

3. Did father go to bed?

4. Did father see you?

5. Did you see mother?

6. Does she see father?

7. How is your sister?

8. Do you like vegetables?

9. Where is the lettuce?

10. Where are the potatoes?

11. Where is your lunch?

12. Please get the onions.

13. Do you like eggs?

14. Yes, I like candy very much.

15. Do you want this cereal?

16. Yes, thanks very much.

17. What fruits do you like?

18. Do you eat many vegetables?

19. What vegetables do you like?

20. What do you want to drink?

21. Did you see the cake?

22. I didn't see the corn on the table.

23. I want some more bread.

24. Do you eat much fish?

25. Do you want more meat?

26. I ate the spinach.

27. Do you want some radishes?

28. Please put the squash, beans, and carrots on the table.

29. Go get the toast.

30. Father wants some more tomatoes and cucumbers for the salad.

31. My brother likes cookies and candy.

32. Do you want ice cream on your pie?

33. He went home for dinner.

34. It's time to eat breakfast.

35. What time is supper?

36. Do you want a snack?

37. What's for breakfast?

Lesson 4. Colors, time, pets, playtime

1.	at	26.	paper
2.	be	27.	pen
3.	big	28.	pencil
4.	bird	29.	pink
5.	black	30.	play
6.	blue	31.	purple
7.	book	32.	quiet
8.	brown	33.	read
9.	cat	34.	red
10.	calendar	35.	sit
11.	clock	36.	small
12.	color	37.	sofa
13.	doll	38.	tan
14.	dog	39.	telephone
15.	down	40.	television
16.	game	41.	today, day
17.	green	42.	tomorrow
18.	have, has, had	43.	tonight
19.	in	44.	toy
20.	just	45.	white
21.	little	46.	with
22.	magazine	47.	write
23.	minute	48.	yellow
24.	newspaper	49.	yesterday
25.	o'clock	50.	-ly

Practice Sentences

1. What color is your pencil?

2. This pen is green.

3. It's not red.

4. It's not purple or yellow.

5. Is this dog yours?

6. That's his little cat, not mine.

7. Are these apples yellow?

8. No, they're not yellow. They're red.

9. Are those dogs white?

10. No, they're not white. They're brown.

11. I have a good tan. Do you?

12. Do you want some oranges?

13. Do you want black coffee?

14. Is that bird pink?

15. Are you going to the game tonight?

16. Please be quiet.

17. Please play quietly with your toys.

18. Do you want to go to the game?

19. Is this your doll?

20. Do you want to play a game?

21. Please sit down.

22. Where did you see the calendar?

23. My big brother and your little sister are reading a book.

24. He has a big green sofa at home.

25. Do you like television these days?

26. I want some magazines and newspapers.

27. What time is it?

28. She has a small blue clock.

29. It's seven o'clock in the morning.

30. It's ten o'clock at night.

31. Just a minute.

32. Please write your name on this paper.

33. Do you like to read?

34. The cat wants some milk.

35. What color is your dog?

Lesson 5. Clothing, some adjectives, will-would

1.	bad	26.	robe
2.	bar	27.	right
3.	beauty	28.	sad
4.	belt	29.	shirt
5.	blouse	30.	shoe
6.	boot	31.	skirt
7.	can't	32.	sleep
8.	cap	33.	slip
9.	chocolate	34.	sock
10.	clothes	35.	stocking
11.	coat	36.	suit
12.	dress	37.	sweater
13.	give	38.	tie
14.	happy	39.	towel
15.	hat	40.	ugly
16.	hate	41.	vest
17.	jacket	42.	was
18.	love	43.	washcloth
19.	lovely	44.	were
20.	me	45.	will
21.	new	46.	would
22.	old	47.	wrong
23.	pajamas	48.	young
24.	pant	49.	-ful
25.	pretty	50.	-y

Practice Sentences

1. Will you be at home tomorrow?

2. Would you like some candy?

3. Please give me a candy bar.

4. Do you want some chocolate cake?

5. I hate chocolate milk.

6. That is a pretty dress.

7. Do you want a cookie?

8. What color are your shoes?

9. Please get your towel and washcloth.

10. You are wrong and he is right.

11. Are you happy?

12. No, I'm not happy. I'm sad.

13. Is that coat old?

14. No, it's not old. It's new.

15. Please get your slip, blouse, and skirt.

16. I like your lovely new sweater.

17. I'm sleepy. I want to go to bed.

18. Don't be bad!

19. That's my jacket, not yours.

20. Where are your shoes and socks?

21. Do you like my new pant suit?

22. Yes, it's beautiful.

23. I hate my pajamas. They're ugly.

24. Were you bad?

25. No, I was good.

26. Please get your cap, coat, and boots.

27. Will you give me some cookies?

28. I like chocolate cake, and I love chocolate candy.

29. I can't go to sleep.

30. I like black coffee.

31. My mother has a new hat.

32. Where are father's belt and tie?

33. I hate this old cap.

34. I want some new stockings.

35. Would you put on your new shirt and vest, please?

Lesson 6.   Prepositions, furniture, rooms

1.	able, -able	26.	floor
2.	above	27.	from
3.	after	28.	garage
4.	age	29.	here
5.	all	30.	house
6.	always	31.	kitchen
7.	angel	32.	lamp
8.	any	33.	never
9.	another	34,	off
10.	area	35.	other
11.	around	36.	over
12.	as	37.	place
13.	back	38.	refrigerator
14.	bake	39.	room
15.	bath	40.	rug
16.	before	41.	school
17.	begin	42.	sink
18.	below	43.	stove
19.	bike	44.	there
20.	block	45.	till
21.	ceiling	46.	toilet
22.	cook	47.	tub
23.	couch	48.	under
24.	curtain	49.	wall
25.	dine	50.	work

Practice Sentences

1. Do you want to go around the block?
2. What is the age of that couch?
3. I'm able to do that.
4. Are all mothers beautiful?
5. Do you want another cup of coffee?
6. This area is all yours.
7. Please put your bike in the garage.
8. Mother's not here this morning.
9. She's at my sister's house till tommorow.
10. Are you baking a chocolate cake?
11. We are beginning to be able to do it.
12. Do you want a bath?
13. Where is your bedroom lamp?
14. I don't like to cook.
15. Put the paper on the wall, please!
16. Mother always puts curtains at the windows.
17. Put the dishes in the sink.
18. She is as bad as you are.
19. The clock is above the table.
20. I don't have any milk, sorry!
21. Do you know his other name?
22. There are five cats on the kitchen floor.
23. We will never get there from here.
24. It's on the table under the window.
25. That stove and refrigerator are new.
26. Put the rug in the tub.
27. He put her dog in the toilet at school.
28. Their place is below ours.
29. Where will you dine tomorrow night?
30. The dining room ceiling is beautiful.

Lesson 7. More family and time words, vehicles, can-could, may-might

1.	aunt	26.	late
2.	baby	27.	man, men
3.	birth	28.	may
4.	boat	29.	might
5.	boy	30.	mom
6.	bus	31.	moment
7.	by	32.	month
8.	can	33.	next
9.	car	34.	plane
10.	child	35.	ship
11.	children	36.	sick
12.	could	37.	sometimes
13.	cousin	38.	son
14.	cute	39.	soon
15.	dad	40.	train
16.	daughter	41.	truck
17.	dear	42.	uncle
18.	early	43.	us
19.	end	44.	week
20.	finish	45.	when
21.	girl	46.	woman, women
22.	grandfather	47.	year
23.	grandmother	48.	-en
24.	hour	49.	-ness
25.	last	50.	'll

Practice Sentences

1. That dog is lovable.
2. My aunt gets carsick.
3. Please read this paper for me.
4. He came on the bus.
5. This book was written by my father.
6. This toy boat is for you.
7. Can you bake a cake for us?
8. Do you want to go on the train?
9. Where does your plane stop?
10. Could you finish that work tomorrow?
11. May my grandmother see your baby sister?
12. Will you get some chalk for me?
13. How many children do you have?
14. He'll be back in an hour--pretty late.
15. His uncle is coming on the next ship.
16. Last year was the end of her schooling.
17. Does your son want a cookie?
18. When could I see that child?
19. Her daughter is very sick.
20. Sometimes the children play very quietly.
21. That little boy is cute, isn't he?
22. My dad is going to get me a bike for my birthday.
23. Someday he's going to get me a car.
24. Just a moment, I'll see where my grandfather is.
25. That man's sickness might be over soon.
26. Her cousin wants to meet you early next week.
27. Last month this woman came to see my mother.
28. She's very dear to me.
29. I want a big red truck.
30. Please get in the car and be quiet.

Lesson 8.   Animals, object pronouns, thought words, conjunctions, more prepositions

1.	animal	26.	monkey	51.	've
2.	bear	27.	must		
3.	behind	28.	neither		
4.	break	29.	nor		
5.	bull	30.	or		
6.	but	31.	pig		
7.	camel	32.	remember		
8.	chicken	33.	sheep		
9.	cow	34.	should		
10.	dream	35.	snake		
11.	during	36.	so		
12.	either	37.	them		
13.	elephant	38.	think		
14.	ever	39.	thing		
15.	few	40.	tiger		
16.	find	41.	understand		
17.	forget	42.	us		
18.	front	43.	when		
18.	gorilla	44.	with		
20.	him	45.	while		
21.	hippopotamus	46.	wolf		
22.	horse	47.	wonder		
23.	know	48.	worry		
24.	lion	49.	zebra		
25.	lose	50.	zoo		

Practice Sentences

1. We should eat before we go.
2. Don't lose your cap, it's new.
3. This is a very big elephant.
4. When are we going to the zoo?
5. I got sick during the game.
6. What have you done with that horse?
7. Give those vegetables to the pigs.
8. I think the bear ate your chickens.
9. Either you or your dad must go to find the lost cow.
10. Have you ever seen a lion in a purple car?
11. The gorilla broke the bull's back.
12. I hate snakes, but I like tigers.
13. Did you remember to eat the cake I baked for you?
14. Neither my brother nor I worry much.
15. That monkey is cute.
16. Do you understand your homework?
17. I've got to finish or I'll worry.
18. The wolf wants to find something to eat.
19. Last night I dreamed of eating like a pig.
20. I wonder how the hippo likes fruit.
21. Must we sit in front of the room?
22. She found a few things she liked.
23. Have you ever seen a camel like that?
24. Will you see him before you go?
25. Put the zebra in with the sheep.
26. My sister knows how to get to the zoo.
27. I think the chair is behind the door.
28. I wonder where so many children came from?
29. Don't forget to put the cat out.
30. Do you understand how to do it?

Lesson 9. More adjectives, comparatives

1.	about	26.	light
2.	again	27.	live
3.	ago	28.	long
4.	all	29.	lot
5.	best	30.	luck
6.	better	31.	most
7.	cold	32.	now
8.	cool	33.	quick
9.	dark	34.	short
10.	deaf	35.	slow
11.	easy	36.	small
12.	enough	37.	tall
13.	fast	38.	than
14.	fat	39.	then
15.	hard	40.	thin
16.	hear	41.	tire
17.	hot	42.	too
18.	hurry	43.	wait
19.	hurt	44.	warm
20.	if	45.	won't
21.	large	46.	worse
22.	lazy	47.	worst
23.	least	48.	yet
24.	less	49.	-er
25.	life	50.	-est

Practice Sentences

1. Did that hurt you?

2. Please hurry and finish your work.

3. Don't drink all your milk yet.

4. You can go to hear him if you want to.

5. It's hard to do so much work.

6. Being deaf isn't the worst you could be.

7. He's hard to understand sometimes.

8. Do you like to sleep in a warm or a cold room?

9. This coffee is very hot, don't drink it now.

10. This jacket is too large for me.

11. You'll be late if you don't get up right now.

12. This is the worst news I've ever heard.

13. He is not always this lazy.

14. The less you say about this, the happier I will be.

15. That was the best time I've had yet.

16. Do you think smaller is better?

17. That boy's dog would give his life for the boy.

18. It's not light enough to see yet.

19. Do you like dark meat?

20. That is very tiring work, I won't do much of it.

21. It's been a long time.

22. She thinks thin is beautiful.

23. A long time ago I was very fat; I won't be like that again.

24. Where do you live?

25. You have a lot to be thankful for.

26. Please wait, I'm not in that much of a hurry.

27. Good luck! I know you'll be O.K.

28. She's small enough to get in that window.

29. I'll be lucky again someday.

30. Please get me a large cup of water.

31. The longer you wait, the harder it will be.

32. She's taller than her brother.

33. He's about as short as I am.

34. Have you had enough to eat?

35. Please slow down--I hate to go too fast.

36. Come quick and see the birds.

37. It's easy to think you're always right.

Lesson 10. Food

1.	across	26.	none
2.	almost	27.	nothing
3.	any	28.	once
4.	bacon	29.	pepper
5.	baloney	30.	piece
6.	beef	31.	pizza
7.	biscuit	32.	pop
8.	butter	33.	pork
9.	cheese	34.	rather
10.	clean	35.	roll
11.	coke	36.	salt
12.	cream	37.	sandwich
13.	delicious	38.	sausage
14.	dessert	39.	shake
15.	dry	40.	since
16.	food	41.	spaghetti
17.	french fries	42.	steak
18.	ham	43.	such
19.	hamburger	44.	sugar
20.	hunger, hungry	45.	taste
21.	ice	46.	through
22.	ketchup	47.	twice
23.	mayonnaise	48.	use
24.	mustard	49.	wash
25.	need	50.	which

Practice Sentences

1. I can almost taste my dessert yet.

2. I'd rather have a hamburger than a steak, wouldn't you?

3. Do you want ketchup, butter, mayonnaise, or mustard on your sandwich?

4. He just had a coke and french fries for lunch.

5. Please clean up the kitchen and wash the dishes.

6. I'll dry them for you when I finish my pizza.

7. Do you want a piece of pie or an apple for dessert?

8. Get the ice and put it in the pop, please.

9. I have no salt and pepper for the food.

10. Nothing tastes better than spaghetti to me.

11. Once I had a pineapple milkshake, it was delicious.

12. How about some cream cheese for these biscuits?

13. We had baloney on hard rolls for a light snack.

14. Let's use the sausage, not the bacon, for breakfast.

15. It's almost dinner time, are you hungry?

16. We haven't had anything to eat since yesterday.

17. I think ham tastes twice as good as pork.

18. He slept through dinner last night.

19. Which do you like better, hot dogs or hamburgers?

20. I've never tasted such good food.

Lesson 11. Body parts, verbs

1.	act	26.	leg	51. write
2.	already	27.	mad	
3.	arm	28.	make	
4.	ask	29.	neck	
5.	body	30.	paint	
6.	bother	31.	picture	
7.	choose	32.	pull	
8.	climb	33.	push	
9.	cook	34.	read	
10.	crawl	35.	real	
11.	crayon	36.	run	
12.	cry	37.	say	
13.	dirt	38.	show	
14.	ear, eye, nose	39.	sick	
15.	face	40.	smile	
16.	finger	41.	sore	
17.	fly	42.	stomach	
18.	foot	43.	swim	
19.	hand	44.	tease	
20.	head	45.	throat	
21.	help	46.	toe	
22.	hop	47.	tooth	
23.	instead	48.	try	
24.	jump	49.	walk	
25.	laugh	50.	who	

Practice Sentences

1. Please ask your brother to wash his face.
2. Tell mother I'll walk home from school today.
3. Choose the color you want to paint your room.
4. The little boy made a pretty picture with his crayons.
5. Father teased me and made me laugh.
6. I got something in my eye.
7. Please help me read this book.
8. Do you have a sore throat?
9. Does your stomach hurt?
10. Try to smile instead of crying.
11. Hop over here and climb on the chair.
12. Who will cook supper tonight?
13. He hurt his leg and can't run, so he's mad.
14. Show your father what you made in school.
15. Your neck and ears are dirty, go wash.
16. I've already forgotten who told me that.
17. Get your finger out of my pie!
18. He hasn't a tooth in his head.
19. The baby can already crawl across the room.
20. What did you want to ask your aunt?
21. Give me a hand with this sofa.
22. Push the table over there.
23. She's a real beauty.
24. Some came on foot, some by car.
25. Pull up a chair and sit down.
26. I hate to fly in planes.
27. Why is your brother crying? What's wrong?
28. I can't use these shoes, they make my toes hurt.
29. Who wrote that book you like so much?
30. We really had a good time.

Lesson 12. Miscellaneous

1.	address	26.	people
2.	although	27.	rain
3.	another	28.	round
4.	because	29.	scare
5.	box	30.	season
6.	break	31.	selfish
7.	brush	32.	share
8.	cloud	33.	snow
9.	comb	34.	spring
10.	cut	35.	square
11.	dentist	36.	story
12.	doctor	37.	strong
13.	fall	38.	study
14.	fire	39.	summer
15.	fix	40.	sun
16.	learn	41.	surprise
17.	letter	42.	teach
18.	medicine	43.	test
19.	movie	44.	turn
20.	number	45.	wake
21.	nurse	46.	watch
22.	other	47.	weak
23.	ought	48.	why
24.	own	49.	winter
25.	parent	50.	-self

Practice Sentences

1. Did it scare you when I jumped out?
2. She really surprised me with her selfishness.
3. We ought to make our own beds.
4. Comb your hair and brush your teeth.
5. Please wake your sister, your parents are here.
6. The sun went behind a cloud and it got cold.
7. I like winter better than summer.
8. It's been a very rainy spring.
9. He fell in the snow and broke his leg.
10. Get another chair for your teacher.
11. What other stories do you know?
12. Round glasses are better than square ones on you.
13. Let's watch the movie on TV tonight.
14. I have to see my doctor tomorrow and get some medicine.
15. Write your address and phone number on this paper, please!
16. Some people never study for tests.
17. I'll write a letter to tell her why I'm not going.
18. It's my turn to fix dinner tonight.
19. I came because I wanted to see the nurse.
20. There's a box for you on the table over there.
21. I'll go, although I don't want to.
22. That's pretty strong medicine for a weak child.
23. I used to want to be a fireman.
24. He told me he did it himself.
25. I watched myself get fatter and fatter.

Lesson 13. More places

1.	bank	26.	museum
2.	beach	27.	office
3.	become	28.	park
4.	between	29.	plant
5.	block	30.	pool
6.	build	31.	promise
7.	bush	32.	river
8.	class	33.	road
9.	college	34.	same
10.	differ	35.	sea
11.	dumb	36.	seem
12.	earth	37.	send
13.	far	38.	shop
14.	flower	39.	side
15.	follow	40.	sky
16.	grass	41.	smart
17.	grow	42.	star
18.	hospital	43.	station
19.	lake	44.	stay
20.	let	45.	still
21.	library	46.	store
22.	look	47.	street
23.	market	48.	tree
24.	moon	49.	-ent
25.	mountain		

Practice Sentences

1. You look a lot like your sister.
2. We live on the next street between the park and the hospital.
3. Please stay off the road when you're not well.
4. I'd rather be at the beach than in the mountains.
5. We'll send the children to the store for the bread.
6. Father works at the office building a block from the museum.
7. Follow me through the trees to the garden.
8. None of the flowers I planted are growing this year.
9. Let's go shopping at the new stores tomorrow.
10. I forgot my coat in the train station.
11. We should stop at the bank before going to the lake.
12. Is the moon still big and yellow tonight?
13. Promise me you'll write a letter today.
14. The stars are all over the sky.
15. I want to stay at the pool a little longer.
16. It's really different to be outside far from home.
17. My brother goes to the library twice a week.
18. Can you see the cat under the bushes watching that bird?
19. Someday I'll go to sea on a ship.
20. You'll become very sick if you eat many more green apples.
21. My sister seems much happier since her son came home.
22. Earth, sun, and water make things grow well.
23. I hate to think of four years of college.
24. She's the smartest girl in our class.
25. That was really a dumb thing for me to do.

Lesson 14. More of this and that . . .

1.	among	26.	kid
2.	bright	27.	money
3.	buy	28.	penny
4.	camp	29.	save
5.	cent	30.	sell
6.	change	31.	spend
7.	Christmas	32.	stamp
8.	clear	33.	sure
9.	dollar	34.	sweetheart
10.	each	35.	syrup
11.	electric	36.	take
12.	empty	37.	talk
13.	every	38.	Thanksgiving
14.	false	39.	true
15.	feel	40.	turkey
16.	fight	41.	unless
17.	friend	42.	until
18.	full	43.	vacation
19.	gas	44.	way
20.	gift	45.	wife
21.	give	46.	word
22.	govern	47.	-ence
23.	Halloween	48.	-ity, -icity
24.	holiday	49.	-ment
25.	husband	50.	-th

Practice Sentences

1. My husband bought me a new car for Christmas.

2. Be sure to give my love to your mother.

3. I feel as if I'm among real friends.

4. We're going to spend our holiday in the mountains.

5. Every dollar must be saved for our vacation.

6. How many cents is a stamp these days?

7. Wait here until I come back with the other kids.

8. It's a clear night, all the stars are very bright.

9. He said his wife was making a gift for us.

10. I won't go unless you come too.

11. I want you to hear every word he has to say.

12. Can't you make the kids stop fighting?

13. What's the difference between a friend and a sweetheart?

14. My mother uses syrup on the turkey at Thanksgiving.

15. Where can I buy something to give the children at Halloween?

16. All he can talk about is what's wrong with the government.

17. We surely used a lot of electricity this winter.

18. Are you going to sell your house to him?

19. Have you ever gone camping on the beach?

20. Do you have change for a dollar?

21. I ate so much I'm really full.

22. I think the tank is empty--we need gas.

23. What's the best way to spend a rainy day?

24. I'd like to go for a walk with my friends.

25. Her sweetheart told her she's the girl of his dreams.

26. It's false that he doesn't know how to tell the truth.

BEGINNING CURRICULUM B SIGNING EXACT ENGLISH

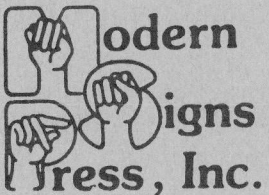

Modern Signs Press, Inc.

This section of the student workbook for Beginning Curriculum B of Signing Exact English includes vocabulary lists, practice phrases, practice sentences, and paragraphs for the 24 lessons which contain approximately 720 words and affixes.

CURRICULUM B, LESSON 1

1.	a	16.	I
2.	am	17.	is
3.	and	18.	it
4.	are	19.	me
5.	ball	20.	mother
6.	boy	21.	my
7.	come	22.	shoe
8.	do	23.	the
9.	father	24.	to
10.	girl	25.	want
11.	give	26.	what
12.	good	27.	where
13.	happy	28.	with
14.	have	29.	you
15.	hello	30.	your

Practice Sentences

1. I have a ball.
2. I am happy.
3. Father and Mother are happy.
4. Give the ball to the boy.
5. Come with me.
6. What do you want?
7. Father is with you.
8. The girl is happy.
9. I have the shoe.
10. Hello!
11. I want my mother.
12. Is it my father?
13. Give it to me.
14. My mother is good.
15. Where is my shoe?
16. I want to give it to you.
17. What do I have?
18. Where is it?
19. You are with Father.
20. You are with your mother.

Receptive Paragraphs

My mother is happy. My father is happy. I am with my mother and father. I am a happy girl.

Hello! I am a good boy. What do I have? I have a shoe. I want to give it to you.

Where is father? Come with me, father. I have a ball. Is it your ball? Father and I have it. Where is my ball?

You are happy. You are a good girl. You are a good boy.

What do you want? I want you to come with me. I want father and mother to come with me. I want the boy and girl to come with me. Do you want to come?

1.	baby	16.	hers
2.	big	17.	him
3.	blue	18.	his
4.	book	19.	ice cream
5.	brown	20.	little
6.	cat	21.	no
7.	chair	22.	not
8.	cookie	23.	on
9.	ear	24.	please
10.	eat	25.	put
11.	eye	26.	see
12.	has	27.	she
13.	hat	28.	yes
14.	he	29.	-ing
15.	her	30.	-s

Practice Phrases

1. Good girl.
2. Good boy.
3. Yes, please.
4. Big girl.
5. Big boy.
6. Please eat.
7. Please come.
8. No, no, no.

Practice Sentences

1. The baby eats the cookie.
2. Please give him the book.
3. The cat is big.
4. The blue hat is hers.
5. The book is on the chair.
6. See her brown cat.
7. Yes, she eats ice cream.
8. The little girl wants her mother.
9. I see my ball.
10. Put the shoe on the chair.
11. I am giving it to you.
12. No, he eats with me.
13. Father has blue eyes.
14. What are you eating?
15. Do you see his ear?
16. The cookie is good.
17. I am coming.
18. Please come to me.
19. Where is your eye?
20. Eat your cookie, and I have a book to give you.

Receptive Paragraphs

Mother wants you. She wants you to come. You have her hat, her brown hat. You put it on your chair. Where is the hat? Mother wants her hat.

The little boy has brown hair. He has blue eyes. Do you see him? He is the boy on the chair. He is not the baby.

I see a cat. Mother, do you see it? Is it brown? Yes, mother sees it, and it is brown. It is eating my ice cream. No, do not eat my ice cream.

He has his book. I have my book. He is happy with his book, and I am happy with my book. The baby is not happy. She wants to have a book. He gives his book to her. She is happy with his book.

CURRICULUM B, LESSON 3

1. an	15. of
2. apple	16. our
3. be	17. ours
4. bed	18. red
5. cup	19. table
6. dog	20. thank
7. drink	21. time
8. find	22. toy
9. go	23. us
10. had	24. was
11. here	25. water
12. in/out	26. we
13. kitchen	27. were
14. milk	28. -ed, or past tense
15. mine	29. -en, or past participle

Practice Phrases

1. Come in.	6. Here we go.
2. Thank you.	7. Thanks.
3. Time to go.	8. Go on.
4. No, thank you.	9. Yes, you are.
5. Time to eat.	10. Here we are.

Practice Sentences

1. He went to bed.

2. We were on time.

3. What were you doing?

4. Mother gave us an apple.

5. The dog had been drinking water.

6. She has a red cup.

7. I have a brown dog.

8. What did he drink?

9. We found her little toy.

10. Please go to bed.

11. Our kitchen is where we eat.

12. We can find him in here.

13. The red toy is mine.

14. Give her a cup of milk.

15. Is it his?

16. The kitchen table is brown.

17. Please thank Mother and Father.

18. Does he want her ice cream?

19. Put the toy dog on the chair.

20. I want a cup of milk to drink and an apple to eat.

Receptive Paragraphs

The red apples were in the kitchen. Mother and I gave little apples to the boys. I ate mine. We were happy.

We had cups to drink water. We put ours on the table. We had to find the brown table and the blue chairs. The table was in the kitchen. We saw where it was. It was time to go.

The toy was on the blue bed. We had it here. Mother saw it on the chair. Where did you find it? The little boy was happy you came to find it. He wanted the toy.

CURRICULUM B, LESSON 4

1.	at	16.	queen
2.	down	17.	sit
3.	green	18.	stand
4.	hear	19.	stop
5.	jeans	20.	their
6.	look	21.	theirs
7.	love	22.	them
8.	many	23.	there
9.	new	24.	they
10.	noise	25.	this
11.	now	26.	three
12.	one	27.	two
13.	pants	28.	up
14.	people	29.	who
15.	plane	30.	zoo

Phrases

1.	Please stand up.	6.	Stop them.
2.	Look up.	7.	Look here.
3.	Please stop.	8.	How many?
4.	Sit up.	9.	Who is it?
5.	Sit down.	10.	Not now.

Practice Sentences

1. Stop at the zoo.
2. Look at the new queen.
3. Do you hear me?
4. I hear many noises.
5. Who has green jeans?
6. Come down now!
7. They are new people here.
8. Who put up the toy plane?
9. They were standing with the new queen.
10. We were up there.
11. Give the pants to him.
12. We loved the water.
13. The three boys want their milk.
14. One of them is here now.
15. This is our plane.
16. Sit upon this chair.
17. Many of them were here.
18. Find the two girls.
19. Stand up and look at the zoo.
20. The new baby is theirs.

Receptive Paragraphs

Look at this. This is my new toy plane. Do you see it? It is red and green. Do you see the little people sitting in my plane? How many do you see? There they go, up, up, up. I hear the noise of my toy plane. I love my new toy.

We are sitting in the kitchen. You are drinking your cup of milk. He is eating his cookie. I am eating an apple. How many people are in the kitchen? I see three people. One, two, three.

The Queen wanted to go to the zoo. She had been there one time. She loved to go to the zoo. Did she see a dog and a cat at the zoo? No, she did not.

I have new pants. They are jeans. Mother gave the jeans to me. They are not blue jeans. They are green. Thank you, mother. I love my new green jeans.

1.	bird	16.	how
2.	cake	17.	light
3.	can	18.	make
4.	car	19.	off
5.	climb	20.	old
6.	color	21.	play
7.	five	22.	ride
8.	for	23.	shirt
9.	four	24.	six
10.	from	25.	that
11.	get	26.	wait
12.	goodbye	27.	will
13.	grandfather	28.	yellow
14.	grandmother	29.	-er
15.	horse	30.	-est

Phrases

1.	Hello!	6.	Four, five, six.
2.	Goodbye.	7.	Put it down.
3.	How are you?	8.	Up you go.
4.	Please stop that!	9.	Climb up.
5.	Get up now.	10.	I will.

Practice Sentences

1. I saw six red birds.
2. Will your mother make a cake?
3. The boy climbed on the brown horse.
4. What color is your car?
5. There are five yellow balls.
6. They are waiting for us.
7. Four boys are playing with them.
8. Please get the blue shirt for me.
9. Grandfather and Grandmother are coming to see me.
10. How did they do that?
11. The light is off.
12. My mother made two cakes.
13. How old are you?
14. How many people went to the zoo?
15. The queen will stand up now.
16. Does my yellow shirt go with blue jeans?
17. His toy is newer.
18. He has the biggest horse.
19. What color is the plane?
20. The boy put on his shirt and pants.

Receptive Paragraphs

We went to see Grandfather and Grandmother. They are not old. They love to play with me. Grandfather played ball with me. Grandmother helped me make a cake. I love Grandfather and Grandmother.

Father has a new car. It is blue. It is light blue. I can ride in the new car. Four of us can ride in the car. It is a little car.

I want to go to the zoo. There are birds at the zoo. I want to see the red and green birds. How many birds are there in the zoo? There are many. One, two, three, four, five, six. I see six birds now. There are many birds at our zoo.

1.	alligator	16.	nine
2.	black	17.	pan
3.	bowl	18.	seven
4.	cereal	19.	some
5.	child (children)	20.	spoon
6.	coat	21.	take
7.	cold	22.	these
8.	dress	23.	toilet
9.	eight	24.	truck
10.	elephant	25.	turn
11.	finish	26.	under
12.	hot	27.	watch
13.	listen	28.	white
14.	man (men)	29.	why
15.	must	30.	woman (women)

Phrases

1.	Turn if off.	6.	Help me.
2.	Put it down.	7.	Watch me.
3.	Look at that.	8.	Do it now.
4.	What are these?	9.	Why?
5.	What color is it?	10.	Seven, eight, nine.

Practice Sentences

1. Our zoo has six alligators and eight elephants.
2. His new car is black and white.
3. The children want three bowls of cereal.
4. Mother gave me a new coat.
5. Is that cereal cold?
6. The girl has a red dress.
7. Did you finish eating your hot cereal?
8. Listen to that noise!
9. The men and women took a ride in the car.
10. I must go now.
11. There are nine trucks.
12. The baby is playing with a pan and a spoon.
13. Seven children came to see me.
14. Some of us can help you do it.
15. Do you want me to take this one?
16. These trucks and cars are old.
17. Where is the toilet?
18. Turn off the light, please.
19. The white cat is watching the black dog.
20. Why is she sitting under the chair?

Receptive Paragraphs

The little boy and girl came to see us. They wanted to play with some children. They had some toys. They had toy trucks and cars. We played with them. We ate some cereal. We finished playing, and they took their toys to their mother.

It is cold. I have a new coat. Mother wants to dress me for the cold. She put on my dress. She put on my new coat. Will I be hot? No, I will not be hot. It is cold.

Father took us to the zoo. We saw many birds, cats, alligators, and elephants. We did not take our dog to the zoo. We did not see a dog at the zoo. We watched a man give hot cereal to the elephants. We watched the elephants eat. I love elephants. They are big. I listened to the elephants. Children love to go to the zoo. Thank you, father, for taking us to the zoo.

CURRICULUM B, LESSON 7

1. bath	16. lunch
2. boat	17. orange
3. breakfast	18. pajama
4. comb	19. soap
5. cook	20. television (T.V.)
6. cow	21. ten
7. cracker	22. those
8. dinner	23. tree
9. dirt	24. tub
10. drum	25. twelve
11. eleven	26. walk
12. face	27. wash
13. fish	28. which
14. hair	29. -ly
15. Indian	30. -y

Phrases

1. Lunch time.	6. Please wash.
2. Time to go.	7. Wash your face.
3. Cowboys and Indians.	8. Ten, eleven, twelve.
4. In and out.	9. Dinner time.
5. Up and down.	10. Crackers and milk.

Curriculum B, Lesson 7, cont'd

Practice Sentences

1. It is time to take your bath.
2. You can play with your toy boat.
3. Please wash your face and comb your hair.
4. Is there hot water in the bath tub?
5. Her face was dirty.
6. Did you wash your hair with soap?
7. Which of us is going to cook breakfast?
8. I had an orange for lunch.
9. Father had crackers with his dinner.
10. Do you want to watch T.V.?
11. Indians eat fish for dinner.
12. The little boys played cowboys and Indians.
13. Did you hear them play the drums?
14. There were nine cowboys and ten Indians.
15. I saw them climb the tree.
16. He put on his pajamas.
17. Eleven people watched T.V.
18. Put out the cat and turn off the lights.
19. Those children walked with me.
20. I want to go for a walk.

Receptive Paragraphs

Dinner was finished. I wanted to watch T.V. I wanted to see the cowboys and Indians. Father wanted me to take my bath. I got my pajamas and went to take my bath. I put hot water in the bath tub. I got in the water with my toy boat. I played with the red and black boat. I washed my dirty face and hair. I put on my pajamas and combed my hair. Father was watching T.V. I watched T.V. with him.

Did you hear the Indians? There were ten little Indians. They were playing their drums. They went to find some water. They wanted to go fishing. They got twelve fish. They cooked the fish and gave some to the cowboys. They had a good dinner.

Grandmother and grandfather had twelve children. Those children are now men and women, and they have many children. My mother and father have two children, a boy and a girl. I am that girl, and I have two children, a boy and a girl. I want to be a grandmother. Will I be a good one?

69

1.	away	16.	monkey
2.	banana	17.	pick
3.	brother	18.	pink
4.	candy	19.	push
5.	clean	20.	say
6.	doctor	21.	sick
7.	doll	22.	sister
8.	duck	23.	sleep
9.	fun	24.	sweater
10.	giraffe	25.	swing
11.	house	26.	talk
12.	juice	27.	telephone
13.	jump	28.	tell
14.	like	29.	wake
15.	may	30.	when

Practice Phrases

1.	Go away.	6.	Put it away.
2.	Get up.	7.	Talk to me.
3.	Wake up.	8.	Brother and sister.
4.	Go to sleep.	9.	Mother and father.
5.	Clean it up.	10.	Push me please.

Practice Sentences

1. Please tell him to put away his toys now.
2. My brother ate a banana and an orange for breakfast.
3. Children like candy.
4. When you are sick, you go to a doctor.
5. Is your face clean?
6. Her father made a dollhouse for her.
7. The little duck was white.
8. The monkey looked funny, jumping up and down.
9. They saw the monkeys and the giraffes at the zoo.
10. My mother likes orange juice for breakfast.
11. May I please have that pink sweater?
12. What could I say on the telephone?
13. Do you like the colors pink and green?
14. He pushed his sister in the swing.
15. The baby is sleeping now.
16. I talked to grandmother and grandfather on the telephone.
17. It is time to wake up.
18. When do you want to eat lunch?
19. People are fun to watch.

Receptive Paragraphs

I woke up at breakfast time. I was not happy. I was sick. I was hot. Mother talked to my doctor. My doctor was not happy that I was sick. He wanted me to sleep. I do not want to be sick. I am going to sleep now.

There are fifteen children at my house. We are going to play. Some children have dolls, some have boats, some have balls, and some have toy ducks. I want to play house. We can play with my new dollhouse. My sister has a doll swing and a doll telephone. We will have fun playing house.

My brother and I went to the zoo with our mother and father. We wanted to see the new giraffes and monkeys. When we went to the monkey house, the monkeys were eating breakfast. They had bananas and oranges. When they finished eating, the monkeys played. They jumped and climbed and ran. I like the monkeys. My brother likes the giraffes. They are big and brown and yellow. They did not jump and climb and run. They stood there and ate. They stood there and slept. We had fun at the zoo.

CURRICULUM B, LESSON 9

1. animal	16. mom
2. blanket	17. more
3. box	18. move
4. bread	19. open
5. break	20. pull
6. care	21. rain
7. chick (chicken)	22. room
8. close (verb)	23. round
9. dad	24. run
10. door	25. sock
11. dry	26. soft
12. egg	27. sun
13. food	28. tell
14. full (-ful)	29. warm
15. hand	30. wet

Phrases

1. Be careful.	7. Open and close.
2. Mom and Dad.	8. Black and white.
3. Run around.	9. In and out.
4. Go out and play.	10. Up and down.
5. Tell me.	11. Wet and dry.
6. Push and pull.	12. Hot and cold.

Practice Sentences

1. How many animals do you see?
2. The baby has her pink blanket.
3. The little boy has a white toy box in his room.
4. Mother made bread for our lunch.
5. Be careful not to break your new toy.
6. We ate eggs for breakfast and chicken for dinner.
7. Please close the door.
8. Daddy and Mommy pushed us in the swings.
9. Are your hands wet or dry?
10. Fish, chicken, and eggs are good foods.
11. There was a roomful of people at our house.
12. Mom has warm, soft hands.
13. Open the box and put your toys away.
14. They have moved to a bigger house.
15. Are there more animals in the zoo now?
16. He pulled on the door, and it opened.
17. It is rainy and wet.
18. He ran around the house with his dog.
19. She told him to put on his socks.
20. It is sunny and warm now.

Receptive Paragraphs

Mother washed my shirt, socks, and blanket. They are not dry. It is time for me to go to sleep. I want my soft blanket. Mother, is it dry? Yes, it is dry. She put it in my room.

We are going to move. My mother and father wanted a new house. There are eight people, and we all want a room. Father found a bigger house for us. It has rooms for eight people, and we will be happy in our big house.

Mother told me to go out to play. It is warm and sunny. It is not raining. I put on my coat and opened the door. I saw my cat playing with a ball. I ran to play with my black and white cat. I did not close the door. Mother did not care. She saw that I was having fun.

CURRICULUM B, LESSON 10

1.	again	16.	key
2.	all	17.	late
3.	arm	18.	leg
4.	block	19.	let
5.	blow	20.	name
6.	body	21.	night
7.	build	22.	nose
8.	clock	23.	over
9.	cry	24.	show
10.	day	25.	side
11.	fall	26.	snow
12.	feel	27.	wind
13.	glass	28.	work
14.	hold	29.	o'
15.	hurt	30.	's

Numbers 1-100

Practice Phrases

1.	Show me.	6.	Do is again.
2.	Hold it.	7.	It hurts.
3.	Look over there.	8.	All of it.
4.	Where is it?	9.	Let's go.
5.	What time is it?	10.	Night and day.

Practice Sentences

1. Build it for me again.
2. All of us want to see the show again.
3. She broke her arm and leg.
4. Build it with the blocks.
5. The wind is blowing now.
6. That body has four legs.
7. It is five o'clock at night.
8. The baby cried when it fell down.
9. Today it is windy and snowy.
10. How does he feel now?
11. Hold the glass carefully.
12. Was the baby hurt when he fell?
13. I put the key over there.
14. All of them were late today.
15. Let me help you build with the blocks.
16. What is the name of the workman?
17. The baby showed me his nose.
18. When the sideshow was over, we went home.
19. The baby's cup is broken.
20. They went to work at 8 o'clock.

Receptive Paragraphs

Let's go to the show tonight. Please pick me up at eight. I want to go with our friends. We can walk. Please do not be late. The show is good, and I want to see all of it. The doors open at 8:15. See you later.

The baby is crying. She wants a cup of water to drink. She has been playing with her blocks. She stood up and fell on her toys. She is not hurt. She wants to be with her mother now.

The wind is blowing today. It looks cold outside. I want to play with my brother and sister. Will mother let us play outside on a cold day? I will put on my warm coat. Now it is snowing. Mother said to play inside today. We are playing in our room with our blocks and cars. Later we can play outside in the snow.

CURRICULUM B, LESSON 11

1.	ask	16.	laugh
2.	bacon	17.	or
3.	bear	18.	peach
4.	bring	19.	rabbit
5.	brush	20.	ready
6.	butter	21.	slow
7.	carrot	22.	story
8.	chew	23.	lie (verb)
9.	cut	24.	toe
10.	fast	25.	tomorrow
11.	flower	26.	tooth (teeth)
12.	foot (feet)	27.	towel
13.	grow	28.	window
14.	hamburger	29.	yesterday
15.	hurry	30.	-ly

Practice Phrases

1.	Get up.	6.	Comb your hair.
2.	Sit down.	7.	Watch out.
3.	Stand up.	8.	Be careful.
4.	Go to bed.	9.	Look out.
5.	Brush your teeth.	10.	Get ready.

Practice Sentences

1. Please ask mother to bring it home.
2. We had bacon and eggs for breakfast.
3. Is there a story that tells of a bear and a rabbit?
4. He brushed his teeth after his bath.
5. Chew the carrot carefully.
6. She put butter on the children's bread.
7. The little boy cut the flowers.
8. Put your new socks on your feet.
9. Children grow in a big hurry.
10. Why do they want hamburgers all the time?
11. We can go today or tomorrow.
12. I laughed at the girl's story.
13. Do we want peaches or bananas for dinner?
14. He watched the rabbit eat the carrot.
15. He slowly got ready to go to work.
16. Please tie your shoes now.
17. How many toes do you have?
18. Yesterday the baby cut a new tooth.
19. Dry your face with the yellow towel.
20. They stood at the window and watched the animals play.

Receptive Paragraphs

Tomorrow he is going to make our breakfast. We will have bacon and eggs, orange juice and milk, bread and butter. I don't know how he will do it. He is going to make breakfast for twelve people. He knows he can ask for help. He wants to do all the work. He is growing up.

I am sitting at my window. I can see the animals playing. The flowers are growing. I see a rabbit eating my mother's flowers. Now I see a cat watching the rabbit. Hurry little rabbit. Do not let that cat get you.

They are ready to tell a story. All children love to tell stories. They love to hear stories. What stories do you like? I like stories of animals, and I like stories that tell of people. Will you please tell me a story now?

1.	back	16.	refrigerate
2.	barn	17.	school
3.	crawl	18.	scissors
4.	fence	19.	sheep
5.	floor	20.	sink
6.	gate	21.	sky
7.	grass	22.	star
8.	know	23.	stay
9.	leaf	24.	stove
10.	moon	25.	teach
11.	mouth	26.	try
12.	other	27.	wagon
13.	paper	28.	yard
14.	pea	29.	'm
15.	radio	30.	n't

Practice Phrases

1.	Back up.	6.	School teacher.
2.	Go around.	7.	Stay awake.
3.	Try again.	8.	Open your mouth.
4.	Open the gate.	9.	How many?
5.	Close the door.	10.	Do it again.

Practice Sentences

1. The back of your coat is dirty.
2. He put the animals in the barn for the night.
3. The cat crawled into the box.
4. There is a fence around our house.
5. I don't see it on the floor.
6. The boy tried to open the gate.
7. The grass is growing in our yard now.
8. Do you know how many others are coming to school?
9. Won't it be good to see green leaves again?
10. The moon and stars are in the sky.
11. Open your mouth, and show me your teeth.
12. The teacher gave them paper and scissors.
13. Mother put the peas in the refrigerator.
14. They heard the story on the radio.
15. The sheep ate the grass in the yard.
16. There is a sink, a stove, and a refrigerator in our kitchen.
17. The children wanted to stay awake to see the sun come up.
18. The little boy tried to pull the wagon into the barn.
19. I'm not ready to cut the grass.
20. Do you know who will teach us at school?

Receptive Paragraphs

My friend has a big barn in her backyard. We like to crawl under her fence or jump over her gate to get to the barn. The barn has a dirt floor and many broken windows. One time we brushed many leaves into her toy wagon, took them in the barn, and made a bed out of them. That night we slept on the leaves and looked out the window at the stars and the moon in the sky. We woke up and went into her kitchen in her house. We turned on the radio and opened the refrigerator, looking for something to eat. All that was in there was pea soup and buttermilk. So we got a drink of water from the sink and went back to the barn to bed.

1.	bean	16.	lake
2.	corn	17.	live
3.	cream	18.	mice
4.	drive	19.	mouse
5.	early	20.	onion
6.	farm	21.	pig
7.	feather	22.	rooster
8.	feed	23.	start
9.	fly	24.	swim
10.	fox	25.	than
11.	goat	26.	then
12.	goose	27.	tomato
13.	help	28.	tractor
14.	hen	29.	turkey
15.	keep	30.	very

Practice Phrases

1.	Come early.	6.	Help your mother.
2.	Drive slowly.	7.	Live quietly.
3.	Start now.	8.	Oh, beans.
4.	Please help.	9.	Fly the plane.
5.	Swim very fast.	10.	Help me down.

Practice Sentences

1. The farmer grows beans and corn on his farm.

2. Early in the morning he feeds the chickens and turkeys.

3. The rooster starts the day with his cry.

4. The children find feathers from the old hens.

5. The farmer sells cream and tomatoes.

6. The fox lives by the lake.

7. Sometimes he catches mice and chickens.

8. You should see them fly.

9. The boys like to help drive the tractor.

10. A mouse lives in the barn.

11. He feeds the pigs and then the goose.

12. I like mice better than pigs.

13. Try onions when you cook creamed corn.

14. The boys swim in the lake with the goose and the duck.

15. Go swim. Then you can help your sister.

16. The goat keeps everyone away.

17. Tomatoes and corn are used to feed the pigs.

18. Very soon we will start the truck to drive to the barn.

19. The rooster, and then the hen, flew to the water.

20. You have been a very good helper on the farm.

Receptive Paragraph

The farmer lives by a lake. If you start early, you can see him feed the corn to the pigs and chickens. Drive down to the lake to watch the geese swim. You may find some pretty feathers. The goat and the fox make the old hens fly. The noise from the tractor is heard early in the morning. The farmer needs help with his work. The mice jump into the beans and eat them.

1.	almost	16.	macaroni
2.	better	17.	napkin
3.	broom	18.	pan
4.	but	19.	pass
5.	ceiling	20.	pepper
6.	cheese	21.	plate
7.	daughter	22.	right
8.	dish	23.	roof
9.	family	24.	salt
10.	fork	25.	same
11.	home	26.	small
12.	knife	27.	son
13.	large	28.	sorry
14.	left	29.	vacuum
15.	lie	30.	wall

Practice Phrases

1.	Almost finished.	6.	Say you're sorry.
2.	That's better.	7.	Pass the salt.
3.	Go home.	8.	Lie down.
4.	That's right.	9.	Use your fork.
5.	It's not the same.	10.	Clean your plate.

Practice Sentences

1. My daughter and son are home today.
2. Our family isn't very large.
3. Almost every day I need to vacuum the floor.
4. Our house was built with a large roof.
5. A fly was walking on the ceiling.
6. Be careful with the big knife.
7. My daughter helps me set the table.
8. Put the fork on the left side by the napkin.
9. Place the knife on the right side of the plate.
10. Pass the salt and pepper to your father.
11. My daughter likes her macaroni very hot.
12. Do your work right away. You may want some help.
13. Put the large plate on the table near the wall.
14. Lie down and wait for the family to come.
15. Did you say you were sorry?
16. I am sorry but I did not vacuum the bedroom.
17. She always says the same thing.
18. The dish has too much pepper in it.
19. I'm sorry I broke the broom.
20. Our family went for a walk.

Receptive Paragraph

I am sorry you could not come to see our family. For once we were all home at the same time. Our son and daughter are not small now. We almost had macaroni and cheese for dinner, but I put too much salt and pepper in the dish. The children put the knives, forks, and spoons on the table. We vacuumed and cleaned the ceiling and walls. I must say it was a large job. We all had to lie down and rest, then we felt better. The children looked right and left for you. Sorry you couldn't come.

1.	after	16.	hide
2.	as	17.	loud
3.	because	18.	mad
4.	bike	19.	morn (ing)
5.	both	20.	pocket
6.	by	21.	pop
7.	catch	22.	quiet
8.	count	23.	second
9.	dance	24.	share
10.	every	25.	skate
11.	first	26.	snack
12.	friend	27.	soon
13.	fruit	28.	thing
13.	game	29.	third
14.	gum	30.	trike

Practice Phrases

1.	Don't get mad.	6.	Catch the dog.
2.	Be quiet.	7.	Be my friend.
3.	Try to share.	8.	Count the horses.
4.	Let's dance.	9.	Run and hide.
5.	No more gum.	10.	Not so loud, please.

Practice Sentences

1. Every Saturday and after school some friends come to play.
2. They come to our house on bikes and skates.
3. Sometimes they have a snack in their pocket.
4. My daughter asks for gum and pop.
5. I don't want to make her mad, but I give her fruit.
6. First, they all help find the toys.
7. Second, they make loud noises.
8. Soon things get too quiet. Why are they hiding?
9. Someone is counting to twenty.
10. Wait, they are playing a game.
11. The boys wanted to play catch, but the girls wanted to dance.
12. By 5 o'clock both the girls and boys must go home.
13. The third grade boy started home on his bike.
14. Please don't get mad, everyone must share.
15. Please don't put your gum in your pocket.
16. Count the children, then take them home.
17. As the mother of the family, I try to keep everyone happy.
18. After they went home, we tried to catch a second breath.
19. Please put the trikes and skates away.
20. From now on, we will have friends come two at a time.

Receptive Paragraph

On rainy days both of my children want to play in the playroom. Because they like games, things soon get quiet. Sometimes it's hard to share and someone gets mad. By the middle of the morning we have a snack of cheese and fruit. They'd like to have pop and gum. After the snack is finished, they want to hide. My daughter counts, and my son hides. She always catches him. Things sometimes get loud. A third thing we do is skate. Other days we have friends come or play with the bikes and trikes.

CURRICULUM B, LESSON 16

1. afraid	16. jell (o)
2. bag	17. leave
3. belt	18. lemon
4. blouse	19. money
5. bus	20. much
6. can't	21. near
7. cherry	22. pay
8. cloth (e)	23. penny
9. coffee	24. purse
10. dollar	25. self
11. donut	26. skirt
12. far	27. so
13. hour	28. store
14. if	29. sugar
15. buy	30. Ending: -e

Practice Phrases

1. Not so much.	6. One more penny.
2. More coffee please.	7. So far, so good.
3. Never say can't.	8. By yourself.
4. More money.	9. No sugar please.
5. Not so near.	10. Leave me alone.

Practice Sentences

1. Don't be afraid to go to the store by yourself.
2. It can't be far and the bus stop is near here.
3. If you ride the bus, leave an hour early.
4. You may want a brown bag besides your purse.
5. While you wait, have a donut and coffee.
6. How much money will you need?
7. You will need much more than those pennies.
8. You can't buy a donut for that much money.
9. Wear your blue skirt and a yellow blouse.
10. If you need help, don't be afraid to ask for it.
11. Do you want cherry or lemon jello?
12. Jello has sugar in it.
13. You need to pay the man who works in the store.
14. As you get near home, you may see your friend.
15. The cloth in the store costs five dollars a yard.
16. You may buy a belt to go with your new clothes.
17. The bus came so soon. Did you forget something?
18. Hide your money in your pocket.
19. Count your money after you get back home.
20. Do you want sugar in your coffee?

Receptive Paragraph

One morning I woke up early. I wanted to go to the store to buy a new skirt and blouse. Because the bus was not running, I walked by myself. I took my money in my purse. I looked at so many pretty things, and then I bought a blue skirt and a white blouse. I paid for my new clothes. I had money left, so I bought some coffee and a donut. By that time, the buses were running. So I rode the bus home.

CURRICULUM B, LESSON 17

1. address	16. hard
2. busy	17. kind
3. button	18. lamp
4. call	19. mirror
5. carry	20. next
6. couch	21. paint
7. curtain	22. part
8. days of the week	23. picture
9. desk	24. pillow
10. ease (y)	25. rug
11. fix	26. sheet
12. forget	27. street
13. front	28. teen
14. guess	29. way
15. hang	30. week

Practice Phrases

1. Not next week.	6. Keep quiet.
2. Be kind.	7. Pretty soon.
3. Don't forget.	8. Easy does it.
4. Fix it.	9. Call me later.
5. Look in the mirror.	10. I'm busy.

Practice Sentences

1. Do you live on a busy street?
2. When I call, tell me if you are busy.
3. That kind of lamp is easy to carry.
4. If you push the button, the light will come on.
5. What is the name of your home town?
6. Is the paint on the wall dry?
7. Hang the mirror next to the large desk.
8. The pretty lemon colored curtains hang straight.
9. Don't forget to get the sheets and pillows.
10. Don't be afraid to call the people next door.
11. Part of the rug was cleaned last week.
12. Will you fix the button on the couch?
13. It is hard not to forget what comes next.
14. Monday, Wednesday, and Friday are my busy days.
15. We bought the pillows last Thursday.
16. I guess I bought the right kind of paint.
17. It's not easy to keep your feet off the couch.
18. I do not know which way to go.
19. The streets are so busy on Saturdays.
20. They were as pretty as a picture.

Receptive Paragraph

My brother is moving to a new town. He wants to live in a little house on a quiet street. Next week we will go to that town to help him find his new home. He wants to find it soon so he can fix it up before he goes to work. We will help him paint the rooms when he finds his new address. Think of all the things he will want in his new house. He has a couch, a desk, a bed, and a large rug. He will buy new curtains and pictures. It will be fun to help him fix up his new house.

1.	about	16.	last
2.	above	17.	low
3.	across	18.	matter
4.	age	19.	never
5.	ahead	20.	none
6.	along	21.	nothing
7.	already	22.	only
8.	always	23.	quick
9.	bad	24.	short
10.	best	25.	tall
11.	dark	26.	thin
12.	each	27.	thick
13.	empty	28.	well
14.	heavy	29.	while
15.	high	30.	without

Practice Phrases

1.	Go ahead.	6.	Little or nothing.
2.	Run along.	7.	Never say never.
3.	Above and below.	8.	Thick and thin.
4.	Good and bad.	9.	Each and every one.
5.	High and low.	10.	Short and tall.

Practice Sentences

1. Will you tell us what you know about that matter?

2. The cup is in the cabinet above the counter.

3. They walked across the street to see the black and white dog.

4. It is not polite to ask people their age.

5. Go ahead and see if you can find them.

6. The quick, short man was walking with a tall, thin woman.

7. She has already done the best she could do.

8. It is always dark at night here.

9. Each one of us must be last at some time.

10. While I wasn't looking, the little children emptied the cookie jar.

11. I could not move the heavy rock.

12. He looked high and low for some candy but found none.

13. Last night I read a book while it rained.

14. It doesn't matter to me who is first this time.

15. She has never been quick at knitting, but she does it well.

16. Only those who work at signing learn to do it well.

17. Quickly the short, thick dog jumped over the tall, thin cat.

18. I can do without food while I am busy working.

Receptive Paragraph

It was about ten o'clock at night when I heard a noise above me in the bedroom. I got out of bed and ran across to my brother's room. He is tall and quick, and I wanted him to go ahead of me to see if there was something in the empty room. In the dark, each of us could see nothing. As we climbed the stairs we could hear the noise getting louder. At last we got to the top of the stairs to find the window open and a little cat sitting on the bed playing with a ball. I was happy that it was nothing bigger than that.

1. age	16. hill
2. aunt	17. hole
3. beauty	18. long
4. beaver	19. mountain
5. behind	20. owl
6. belong	21. raccoon
7. between	22. rat
8. bite	23. sad
9. bother	24. skin
10. cousin	25. squirrel
11. cute	26. swan
12. deer	27. uncle
13. forest	28. use
14. frog	29. wolf
15. fur	30. young

Practice Phrases

1. How sad.	6. Soft fur.
2. Up the hill.	7. Don't bite.
3. Don't bother.	8. Far behind.
4. She's cute.	9. Between the trees.
5. Long ago.	10. Use the soap!

Practice Sentences

1. A long time ago I went to the mountains to be with my aunt.

2. My aunt and uncle live in a beautiful house in the forest.

3. Beavers live in the lake behind their house.

4. There are many deer that think they belong there.

5. My cousins and I like to play between the house and the forest.

6. Have you ever watched a beaver bite into a tree?

7. We try not to bother the many animals and their young.

8. My cousins have a cute raccoon that eats from their hands.

9. The fur and skin of forest animals is useful.

10. I like to watch the frogs and the swans on the lake.

11. There are not mountains near my home, only hills.

12. The mountain owl did not catch the rat because he ran to his hole.

13. Yesterday, we went for a long walk, and we saw a wolf.

14. There are wolves in the mountains but no longer do they live near my home.

15. They feed on squirrels and other small animals.

16. As we walked along, we heard the noise of the squirrels.

17. It is more fun to see these animals in the forest than in the zoo.

18. I would like for my family to come to see these beautiful things.

19. After our long walk, we ate dinner while we talked about all the things we had seen.

20. I will feel very sad when I have to leave for home.

Receptive Paragraph

My father and his brothers and sisters grew up in the mountains where they lived daily with beautiful things to see. Each day was new. They learned to be quiet so the animals would not run away. They learned to be careful when they walked around the lake or in the forest. Sometimes animals can be dangerous when they are protecting their young. Now my cousins and I are learning about the mountains from our parents.

1. balloon
2. bell
3. birthday
4. bubble
5. candle
6. choose
7. crayon
8. draw
9. end
10. finger
11. king
12. kiss
13. knee
14. learn
15. number
16. page
17. party
18. present (noun)
19. read
20. remember
21. ribbon
22. silly
23. sing
24. smile
25. tear (verb)
26. tire (verb)
27. together
28. voice
29. wrap
30. write

Practice Phrases

1. The big bell.
2. So many big bubbles.
3. You choose first.
4. The end of the road.
5. Don't be silly.
6. Sing beautifully.
7. Please smile.
8. Are you tired?
9. Quiet voice, please.
10. No more noise.

Practice Sentences

1. Do you know if there will be balloons at his birthday party?

2. They came to the door when they heard the doorbell.

3. All the children brought presents to the birthday party.

4. At the party we can blow bubbles and draw pictures with crayons.

5. There will be five candles on his birthday cake.

6. What kind of present shall we choose to buy for him?

7. While I tie the ribbon, will you hold it with your finger?

8 Children never want their parties to end.

9. The birthday boy is king for the day and can be silly and happy.

10. Do we have to get down on our knees and kiss his hand?

11. We wrote a page of silly stories about kings kissing frogs.

12. All of us learned how to play a new number game.

13. When the birthday boy unwrapped his presents, he tore whem open.

14. He did not bother to untie the ribbons.

15. Before we all got too tired, his mother read us a beautiful story.

16. I will always remember that party because we had fun together.

17. You should have heard all the happy voices singing to him.

18. When it was time to go home, all the children were smiling.

19. We remembered to say thank you for the nice party.

20. If I could choose, I would have a birthday party every day.

Receptive Paragraph

Today is the King's birthday. What do you think he will choose to do? He does not want everyone to go down on their knees and kiss his fingers. He does not want to learn more about reading, writing, drawing and numbers. He wants to have a party with candles on a cake, ice cream and many happy games. He wants to blow up balloons, sing songs, play games, and un-wrap his presents. What kind of presents will people give the King? How about five silver bells, four tree frogs, three pink rabbits, two eggs, and a yellow bird in a green tree?

1. afternoon
2. before
3. boot
4. cage
5. camel
6. change
7. during
8. eagle
9. eve
10. ever
11. fat
12. fill
13. gray
14. hippopotamus
15. just

16. lion
17. midnight
18. measure
19. mix
20. noon
21. pair
22. rest
23. seal
24. shall
25. snake
26. tail
27. tiger
28. trouble
29. turtle
30. zebra

Practice Phrases

1. Forever and ever.
2. Before and after.
3. Good afternoon.
4. Good evening.
5. Just before noon.

6. Again and again.
7. A pair of pants.
8. Measure, then mix.
9. Eat your fill.
10. The rest of the day.

Practice Sentences

1. Before we can go this afternoon, you must take a rest.

2. The zookeeper puts on boots before going into the hippo's cage.

3. Our zoo has camels and zebras, as well as lions and tigers.

4. For some animals, it is better never to change lighting.

5. During the hot days the turtles and snakes stay in the dark.

6. The eagle has a cage all to himself because he is a big bird.

7. In the evening it is fun to watch the seals and hippos eat.

8. The zookeeper mixes their food, measuring very carefully.

9. Those animals have fat on their bodies to keep warm.

10. They are both gray, along with the elephant.

11. It's fun to watch the elephant fill his mouth with his food.

12. There are many pairs of lions who should all have babies soon.

13. Most people don't go to the zoo after midnight.

14. Tomorrow at noon there will be time to pick up snakes and turtles.

15. People have trouble with snakes because they don't know much about them.

Receptive Paragraph

One morning when I was not in school, my mother, father, brother and I went to the new zoo. Mother fixed our lunch so we could stay there all day. It was a sunny day, so we took hats and sunglasses. Our zoo has both farm animals and wild animals. We chose to see only the wild animals. First my brother wanted to look at the big cats. Only the lions and tigers were outside their indoor cages. Then father wanted to see the fat hippopotamus and the seals. Mother walked over to see the camels and zebras, but I ran to see the snakes and turtles. Don't turtles have funny tails? During the afternoon we ate our lunch and then took time to see some of the farm animals. The only trouble was that the goat ate my hat. Evening came too soon, but we can always go back again.

1. airport	16. job
2. apartment	17. kick
3. bank	18. library
4. barber	19. mail
5. basketball	20. movie
6. bridge	21. office
7. church	22. park
8. city	23. picnic
9. country	24. police
10. drug	25. pool
11. film	26. post
12. football	27. restaurant
13. gas	28. river
14. grocer (y)	29. shop
15. hospital	30. station

Practice Phrases

1. Kick the ball.	6. The city park.
2. Football or basketball.	7. The barber shop.
3. The gas station.	8. A drugstore and a grocery store.
4. Let's go shopping.	
5. A picnic in the country.	9. The post office.
	10. The bridge over the river.

Practice Sentences

1. We live in a big city, full of buildings, parks, and houses.

2. The airport is just outside the city, near an office park.

3. City offices are mostly downtown, but there are post offices everywhere.

4. Some people choose to live in apartments with pools.

5. Other people like living near parks, in houses with beautiful yards.

6. There are shops and stores nearby, so people don't have to go far to shop.

7. You can find almost anything you want in a shopping <u>mall</u>.

8. You can get food at a restaurant or grocery store, a haircut at the barber shop, and film at the drugstore.

9. After you shop, you can go to a movie or get books at the library.

10. On the way home you can stop for gas at a gas station.

11. Before you go shopping you go to the bank.

12. After you finish all that, you can play football or basketball.

13. If you get hurt, you can always go to the hospital.

14. Most people get a kick out of going to the country for a picnic.

15. We walked along the river and over the bridge.

Receptive Paragraph

What job will you choose for yourself when you grow up? There are many good jobs in the city or the country. More people work in the cities now. If you want a job helping people, you could be a policewoman or a mailman. You could work in a hospital, church, or library. Barbers, grocers, and bankers are busy people. Some of them have worked at drugstores, restaurants, and gas stations before they chose that job. Some people play football or basketball, which may not sound like a job to you. Whatever your job is, it should make you want to do your best.

1. ant	16. nice
2. bee	17. once
3. believe	18. piece
4. bug	19. plant
5. butterfly	20. poor
6. caterpillar	21. seed
7. delicious	22. spider
8. dig	23. throw
9. fire	24. thumb
10. garage	25. touch
11. garden	26. until
12. honey	27. vegetable
13. lose	28. wear
14. mean	29. web
15. meet	30. worm

Practice Phrases

1. Until then.	6. The spider web.
2. See you later.	7. The honeybee.
3. Lost and found.	8. A vegetable garden.
4. Once upon a time.	9. That's delicious.
5. My green thumb.	10. Believe me!

Practice Sentences

1. There are many ant hills in the garden.
2. Bees come to the red and yellow flowers in our yard.
3. I believe that bugs can be helpful to gardeners.
4. That crawling caterpillar will soon be a beautiful butterfly.
5. Won't these vegetables be delicious on the dinner table?
6. We dug up the yard to plant a vegetable garden.
7. It's fun to cook food over an open fire.
8. We keep our garden tools in the back of the garage.
9. It would be nice to have honey on a piece of bread.
10. I meant to plant some sunflower seeds, but I lost them.
11. Sometimes gardeners meet to talk about new vegetables and other plants.
12. Once in a while the seeds are poor and do not grow well.
13. Try not to touch the spider web because spiders catch other bugs.
14. Don't throw away anything that we might use in the garden.
15. She wears garden clothes until it is time to go to the store.

Receptive Paragraph

Working in the garden can be fun if everyone helps. Each one can do something. Some people like to dig up the garden to make it ready for planting. Others like to plant the seeds in rows. Some people even like to do the weeding. The children like to see the young plants growing because they like to taste all the delicious garden vegetables. Older people seem to be the ones with the green thumbs. It takes lots of hard work and experience to be a good gardener.

CURRICULUM B, LESSON 24

1.	January	16.	summer
2.	February	17.	winter
3.	March	18.	year
4.	April	19.	weather
5.	May	20.	hail
6.	June	21.	ice
7.	July	22.	fog
8.	August	23.	smog
9.	September	24.	cloud
10.	October	25.	map
11.	November	26.	north
12.	December	27.	south
13.	calendar	28.	east
14.	month	29.	west
15.	spring	30.	since

Practice Phrases

1. East and west.
2. Next year.
3. Sunny weather.
4. Month after month.
5. The icy winter.
6. The calendar months.
7. Rain clouds.
8. The March winds.
9. Snowy January.
10. Spring is here.

Practice Sentences

1. January can be a month of ice and snow.

2. February is the month of birthdays of American presidents.

3. March comes in like a lion and goes out like a lamb.

4. April is the first month of Spring here.

5. May is a month of changeable weather and beautiful flowers.

6. June, July, and August are the summer months when it can be hot.

7. School begins in September since the garden and farm work is finished.

8. October brings the Fall of the year when the leaves change colors.

9. November is the month of Thanksgiving.

10. December weather can be icy, foggy, rainy, snowy, or sunny.

11. If you look at a map, you can see that weather is different to the north, south, east, or west of us.

12. It's nice not to have smog when the weather is beautiful.

13. One day we climbed a mountain where it hailed, rained, and snowed on us.

14. I like the changing weather of spring, summer, fall, and winter.

15. Since this is the end of the school year, it must be summertime.

Receptive Paragraph

There are twelve months in the year. Most children go to school for nine months beginning in September. School is over in May for the three months of the summer. During the school year the children have time off in November, December, and March. But the summer is the time of year when the weather is nice, and children like to play outside. Some people go to school in the summer as well as winter, spring, and fall. In some countries the seasons are different. Children seem to like to be outside no matter what the weather.

AFFIXES USED IN SIGNING EXACT ENGLISH

Modern Signs Press, Inc.

This section of the workbook on Affixes used in Signing Exact English is designed for the student who already has a basic command of the SEE vocabulary. A student who has completed one of the beginning curricula in Signing Exact English (either A or B) will find in this workbook approximately 350 additional vocabulary items in addition to the affixes themselves. The sentence structure in the practice sentences in this workbook is somewhat more complex, and the words themselves are at a higher level.

A very important principle to keep in mind when signing these practice sentences is that the prefixes should flow into the sign for the word itself, while suffixes should flow from the sign for the word. Affixes should not be signed with a stress or a pause that separates them from the root word. Be guided by the smoothness of the spoken word. We do not, for instance, say walkING or walk ing.

The student may find a few practice sentences where affixes are practiced which could be signed differently because a sign for the complete word is given in the Signing Exact English text. For instance, "review" may be signed as re+view, or as a basic word with one sign. In such cases the student should be aware that both options are possible, and the choice should depend on what is used in the local program. Consistency is important!

As with the beginning curricula, it is also important that the student understand and incorporate such features of American Sign Language as placement, directionality, negation, question markers, and facial expression. See the section titled, "Points to Remember for Clear, Expressive Signing" in the introduction to the Signing Exact English text for additional information.

AFFIX MOVEMENT CHART

II. Affix movement chart

A.

-an<u>t</u>, -en<u>t</u>
-a<u>ge</u>, -ed<u>ge</u>
-e<u>n</u>ce, -a<u>n</u>ce
-i<u>o</u>n, -ti<u>o</u>n, -<u>s</u>ion
-it<u>y</u>, -icit<u>y</u>
-<u>m</u>ent
-<u>n</u>ess
-<u>u</u>re

B.

-<u>i</u>sm

C.

-<u>o</u>us
-<u>i</u>ng

D.

-<u>a</u>ble, ible
-<u>i</u>st

E.

dis-
<u>i</u>l-, <u>i</u>m-, <u>i</u>r-, <u>i</u>n,
<u>m</u>is-, <u>n</u>on-
<u>u</u>n-

F.

-<u>a</u>te
-<u>i</u>ce
-<u>i</u>le
-<u>i</u>ne
-i<u>t</u>e

G.

-i<u>fy</u>
-<u>i</u>ze

H.

-<u>th</u>
-<u>ee</u>
-<u>e</u>
-<u>ic</u>
-<u>t</u>
-<u>s</u>
-<u>y</u>
-a<u>r</u>
-o<u>r</u>
-e<u>r</u>

I.

-<u>e</u>se
-<u>i</u>sh
-<u>i</u>ve
-<u>ly</u>

J.

anti-

K.

-neath
over-
sub-
under-

Affixes--Practice with the same movement

A. -age, -edge; -ant, -ent; -ence, -ance; -ion, -tion, -sion; -ity, -icity; -ment; -ness; -ure

1. Marriage was the last thing on her mind.

2. What a pleasant afternoon for a long walk in the park.

3. They have different opinions on that subject.

4. Don't underestimate its importance.

5. Absence makes the heart grow fonder.

6. That is a big operation.

7. Please give us your permission.

8. Necessity is the mother of invention.

9. There has been an improvement.

10. Don't mind my nervousness.

11. The legislature will vote next week.

12. There is a shortage of water.

13. The student passed his tests.

14. Did you get your allowance?

15. We want to improve our communication skills.

16. Admission is free.

17. I look for simplicity when planning meals.

18. Our electricity is off.

19. I have an announcement.

20. His carelessness was obvious.

21. Too much exposure to the sun can be dangerous.

22. Please join our association.

A. (continued)

23. <u>Completion</u> of the project took a long time.

24. In <u>addition</u> to washing windows, they had to paint the walls.

25. It was a <u>failure</u>.

26. Her job demands <u>perfection</u>.

27. Is that the correct <u>usage</u> of that word?

28. I am concerned about my child's <u>education</u>.

29. He is looking for <u>employment</u>.

30. That is a difficult <u>situation</u> to be in.

31. Can you smell the <u>fragrance</u>?

32. What is your <u>profession</u>?

33. The dog was known for his <u>gentleness</u>.

34. It is hard to understand the <u>intensity</u> of her pain.

35. Children are <u>dependent</u> on their parents.

36. Have they made an <u>investigation</u>?

B. -a<u>r</u>, -e<u>r</u>, -o<u>r</u>; -<u>e</u>, -<u>ee</u>; -i<u>c</u>; -<u>s</u>; -<u>t</u>; -t<u>h</u>; -y

1. The <u>liars</u> were able to gain a place of influence.

2. These <u>teachers</u> will be taking a leave of absence.

3. I think your <u>behavior</u> has improved.

4. Try to develop a <u>basic</u> sign language vocabulary.

5. The doctor advised me not to <u>bathe</u> the baby until he was well.

6. The baker hired a new <u>employee</u>.

B. (continued)

7. Next month they'll visit some theaters.

8. How much weight have you gained?

9. This is the tenth of December and Christmas vacation begins soon.

10. It's easy to find your way to our home.

11. I left my roller skates on the bus.

12. They're having visitors next week.

13. I don't understand economics.

14. The mailman was not able to find the addressee.

15. Although the cafeteria employees are busy, they always manage to serve our meals on time.

16. Complaints will not be accepted.

17. You must take responsibility for your actions.

18. She is lucky to have survived with only a few injuries.

19. The engineer developed a dramatic plan.

20. I wonder who'll be our next governor.

21. It often becomes windy late in the afternoon.

22. What's the height of the tallest mountain in the world?

23. The student was hungry for more knowledge.

24. We'll be changing residences after January twentieth.

25. What a lousy performance!

26. Get back to basics!

27. My goodness, you were lucky.

28. Both counselors are advising her to study harder.

B. (continued)

29. Those <u>enthusiastic</u> performers put on a spirited show.

30. The principal decided to take the <u>teacher's</u> suggestion under advisement.

31. The <u>width</u> of the river was too far to swim.

32. My husband is <u>crazy</u> about peanut butter and <u>jelly</u> <u>sandwiches</u>.

33. The room was so <u>stuffy</u> she couldn't <u>breathe</u>.

34. <u>Jealousy</u> can make people do <u>things</u> they <u>later</u> regret.

35. I don't have much <u>strength</u> left.

36. A <u>joint</u> committee on <u>youth</u> counseling met last month.

37. It <u>costs</u> a lot of money to feed and <u>clothe</u> children.

C. <u>dis</u>-; <u>il</u>-, <u>im</u>-, -<u>in</u>-, -<u>ir</u>; <u>mis</u>-, <u>un</u>-

1. Her speech seemed <u>disjointed</u>.

2. My parking permit was <u>discontinued</u>.

3. Your reasoning is <u>illogical</u>.

4. They found the TTY to be <u>immovable</u>.

5. Don't be so <u>impatient</u>!

6. Nothing was ever accomplished by <u>inaction</u>.

7. Your assignment is <u>incomplete</u>.

8. Some people are <u>irresponsible</u>.

9. I <u>misspelled</u> some words.

10. They <u>misplaced</u> the costumes.

11. Several of the students are <u>misbehaving</u>.

C. (continued)

12. He <u>miscounted</u> the number of desks.

13. Please don't <u>misuse</u> the books.

14. That was an <u>unpleasant</u> experience.

15. I feel <u>uneasy</u> about finding the survivors.

16. The president is <u>undecided</u> about what action should be taken.

17. She's <u>uncertain</u> about being employed.

18. It's <u>unlikely</u> he'll join the teaching profession.

19. Free admission to the museum is <u>uncommon</u>.

20. The committee decided to <u>disallow</u> my application.

21. They had to return the cloth to the store because of an <u>imperfection</u>.

22. It's <u>impossible</u> to ski in this raging snowstorm.

23. The drug caused <u>irreversible</u> brain damage.

24. It's easy to <u>mismanage</u> your finances.

25. Every mother is thrilled when her child learns how to dress <u>unassisted</u>.

26. We're <u>dissatisfied</u> with the performance.

27. It was an <u>unreasonable</u> demand.

28. The cell was in an <u>immature</u> stage of development.

29. <u>Unemployment</u> is high.

30. I'm so <u>unlucky</u>.

31. His attendance has been <u>irregular</u>.

C. (continued)

32. There's a lot of <u>unimproved</u> land in the area.

33. We <u>misjudged</u> your actions.

34. Your behavior is <u>unacceptable</u>!

35. I <u>misinterpreted</u> the meaning of that word.

36. He was careful to <u>disassociate</u> himself from the group.

37. The film was <u>unexposed</u>.

D. -<u>ese</u>; -<u>ish</u>; -<u>ive</u>; -<u>ly</u>

1. They'll be studying <u>Japanese</u> culture while touring that country.

2. I enjoy watching the <u>Chinese</u> gymnastic team perform.

3. I'm going to take an <u>English</u> course next semester.

4. The <u>Scottish</u> people had a direct influence on <u>Irish</u> history.

5. The <u>Polish</u> population has decreased.

6. He's been so <u>snobbish</u> <u>lately</u>.

7. We visit our <u>Swedish</u> <u>relatives</u> <u>yearly</u>.

8. I'm planning to take a <u>Spanish</u> class.

9. What are the <u>objectives</u> of this educational plan?

10. The cost of new homes is <u>prohibitive</u>.

11. She was the first woman to hold a seat in the House of <u>Representatives</u>.

12. He's been <u>childish</u> about disassociating himself from our group.

13. Thanks for being so <u>supportive</u> in my time of need.

14. Did you know my sister had a <u>progressive</u> disease?

15. I think your suit is very <u>attractive</u>.

16. It will rain tomorrow and <u>possibly</u> the day after.

17. You're <u>partly</u> to blame for the break-up of this marriage.

18. She's been <u>patiently</u> waiting for her opportunity to perform.

19. Do they <u>really</u> believe in elves, fairies and such?

20. Try to figure out the answer to the geometry problem <u>quickly</u>.

21. Our dog has become irritable just <u>recently</u>.

22. Ameslan is <u>commonly</u> called ASL.

23. I <u>rarely</u> have a chance to read for pleasure.

24. He's <u>only</u> <u>friendly</u> with people he knows.

25. Go <u>directly</u> to jail! Do not pass GO!

26. U.S.— Chinese relations have <u>certainly</u> improved.

27. Don't be <u>overly</u> sensitive.

28. Irish handmade sweaters are <u>expensive</u>.

29. Our dog became <u>lonely</u> while we were away on vacation.

30. <u>Japanese</u> cameras are among the most popular.

31. How long will it be before my son can be more <u>physically</u> <u>active</u>?

32. My grandmother is proud of her <u>girlish</u> figure.

33. After a day at the beach his skin was <u>reddish</u>.

D. (continued)

34. Her daughter will have to wear <u>corrective</u> shoes until she's six years old.

35. The <u>detective</u> was hired to investigate the theft.

36. Do you think floods or fires are more <u>destructive</u>?

37. <u>Strangely</u> enough, she's <u>passive</u> in rush hour traffic.

E. -<u>ate</u>; -<u>ice</u>; -<u>ile</u>; -<u>ine</u>; -<u>ite</u>

1. He will <u>officiate</u> at the meeting.

2. I think that story <u>originated</u> with him.

3. The reunion brought back memories of happy <u>collegiate</u> days.

4. An effort is underway to <u>vaccinate</u> all kindergarten age children in this school district.

5. One must learn to be <u>considerate</u> of others to get along in our society.

6. Let's <u>formulate</u> a plan of action to save the whales.

7. Waves lapped at the shore with a <u>pulsating</u> rhythm.

8. The driver education teacher finds it easy to <u>motivate</u> his students.

9. I'm having difficulty <u>motivating</u> my husband.

10. Plans to <u>assassinate</u> the vice president were uncovered.

11. Don't you wonder where that popular phrase <u>originated</u>?

E. (continued)

12. A decision whether or not to <u>activate</u> the reserves rests with the president.

13. Your young cousin is quite <u>opinionated</u>.

14. We received a <u>notice</u> in the mail announcing the opening of a new shopping center nearby.

15. Mom's going to hit the ceiling when she <u>notices</u> the damage to her car.

16. My aunt and uncle prefer this restaurant because of its good <u>service</u>.

17. Funeral <u>services</u> for the mayor are scheduled for Tuesday.

18. Isn't there any <u>justice</u> in this world?

19. The <u>projectile</u> traveled toward its target at an immeasurable speed.

20. That actor certainly has a deep, <u>masculine</u> voice.

21. There are <u>feminine</u> groups who argue pro and con on the Equal Rights Amendment.

22. The doctor will <u>examine</u> you shortly.

23. First semester <u>examinations</u> begin tomorrow.

24. The twins will be playing on <u>opposite</u> teams.

25. Chinese food is my <u>favorite</u>.

26. The clean-cut <u>collegiate</u> look is in fashion.

27. The committee will <u>formulate</u> procedures for licensing <u>service</u> stations.

28. Nature's <u>justice</u> is "survival of the fittest".

29. <u>Opposites</u> attract.

30. In ancient Greek dramas male actors played both <u>feminine</u> and <u>masculine</u> characters.

E. (continued)

31. The rancher and some of his neighbors will <u>vaccinate</u> a herd of cattle this weekend.

32. Tornadoes have been known to throw <u>projectiles</u> through walls of houses.

33. The doctor felt blood <u>pulsate</u> through her veins.

34. Winter is my <u>favorite</u> season because I enjoy winter sports.

35. Did you <u>notice</u> I cleaned my house?

36. This principal demonstrates a sense of <u>justice</u> when counseling students.

37. I'm determined not to become as <u>opinionated</u> as that bachelor.

F. Different movements

-d<u>o</u>m, -est, -ed, -<u>i</u>st, -i<u>fy</u>, -<u>i</u>ze, -<u>n</u>eath, -en
-<u>i</u>ng, -<u>o</u>us, -es<u>s</u>, -<u>i</u>sm, over-

1. I've made an appointment to have my <u>wisdom</u> teeth removed.

2. The queen ruled her <u>kingdom</u> with a sense of justice.

3. Many accidents have <u>occurred</u> on this street.

4. That book is beautifully <u>illustrated</u>.

5. I have <u>been</u> having headaches for quite some time now.

6. He was an <u>unknown</u> writer until late in life.

7. The <u>princess</u> decided to marry a commoner.

8. They hired a <u>governess</u> to teach their children rather than send them to school.

9. I'd like you to meet my <u>best</u> friend.

10. It's the <u>nicest</u> wedding gift they received.

F. Different movements, (continued)

11. Please <u>notify</u> the office of any address change.

12. We will <u>intensify</u> our efforts to find the survivors.

13. It's difficult to <u>criticize</u> her work habits.

14. Your assignment is to <u>summarize</u> this article.

15. This <u>hearing</u> aid battery must be dead.

16. Does she plan on <u>studying</u> medicine?

17. How long do you think his <u>enthusiasm</u> for weight lifting will last?

18. The newly formed country practices <u>socialism</u>.

19. I believe the <u>artist</u> will be selling some of his paintings in the near future.

20. Cell division and fungus growth were the subjects of the <u>biologists's</u> lecture.

21. Most <u>tourist</u> attractions are open on weekends.

22. Let's have our picnic <u>underneath</u> that tree.

23. I know it would be <u>beneath</u> him to cheat on the exam.

24. Those slippery steps are <u>dangerous</u>.

25. Isn't this a <u>marvelous</u> lesson!

26. The young <u>actress</u> <u>reached</u> <u>stardom</u> <u>overnight</u>.

27. It's <u>been</u> <u>threatening</u> to rain all day.

28. If this is the <u>worst</u> thing that's ever <u>happened</u> to you, you're lucky.

29. I am <u>amazed</u> that the little car is so <u>spacious</u>.

30. Use your knowledge of library science to <u>classify</u> these new books.

F. Different movements, (continued)

31. Please send us an <u>itemized</u> list of your medical expenses.

32. The newspaper <u>columnist</u> <u>liked</u> to see his name in print.

33. Do you want this course <u>offered</u> again?

34. Try not to show any <u>favoritism</u>.

35. Have you noticed his strange <u>mannerisms</u>?

36. Who is the tallest <u>student</u> in your class?

37. She often <u>overemphasizes</u> the importance of driving slowly.

G. Different movements

-<u>ante</u>-, <u>pre</u>-; <u>pro</u>-; <u>re</u>-; <u>anti</u>-; <u>inter</u>-; <u>intra</u>-; sub-

1. We were told to wait in the <u>anteroom</u>.

2. The telephone call <u>antedated</u> his written message.

3. Students were <u>preassigned</u> to classes.

4. Dinosaurs populated the earth in <u>prehistoric</u> times.

5. <u>Prefabricated</u> homes are becoming more common.

6. My daughter attends <u>preschool</u> twice a week.

7. The twins were born four weeks <u>premature</u>.

8. He became <u>antisocial</u> as a result of depression.

9. The <u>antiwar</u> demonstrators agreed to meet at the park.

10. She doesn't have enough <u>antibodies</u> to ward off the disease.

11. <u>Interstate</u> highways are the arteries of the trucking industry.

G. Different movements, (continued)

12. My dad's business depends on good <u>international</u> relations.

13. I would like to have more class time for group discussion and student <u>interaction</u>.

14. An <u>intercollegiate</u> basketball tournament was held over the holidays.

15. This watch, which is made up of tiny <u>interlocking</u> pieces, is difficult to repair.

16. The governor favors local and <u>intrastate</u> commerce.

17. The medical student was asked to define the word <u>intravital</u>.

18. <u>Pro-farmer</u> legislation might be passed soon.

19. She has <u>pro-English</u> feelings because of her ancestry.

20. That's a fine <u>reproduction</u> of the original painting.

21. There is nothing like a <u>refreshing</u> glass of ice water on a hot summer day.

22. New England is experiencing <u>subnormal</u> temperatures this winter.

23. Plans for the housing development won't begin until the land has been <u>subdivided</u>.

24. Have you added any <u>antifreeze</u> to the car?

25. She's going to help her aunt and uncle <u>rewallpaper</u> their dining room.

26. I think the traffic <u>interchanges</u> on this freeway were well designed.

27. His mind was <u>preoccupied</u> with his father's illness.

28. Changes in the cell's structure took place over a <u>prolonged</u> period of time.

G. Different movements, (continued)

29. For homework I want you to practice these <u>review</u> sentences.

30. The association had a number of <u>interrelated</u> committees.

31. The storm caused a power failure which was <u>restored</u> within a few hours.

32. Please do not <u>prejudge</u> the issue without hearing both sides.

33. There will be a <u>recount</u> before the winner of the election is announced.

34. Can you identify the <u>pronoun</u> in this sentence?

35. His future career was <u>predetermined</u>.

General practice with AFFIXES

1. You<u>'ve</u> <u>dis</u>honored the family name.

2. I<u>'ll</u> meet you in the <u>ante</u>-room.

3. I<u>'m</u> afraid marriage is becoming <u>out</u>-dated.

4. I<u>'d</u> like to be able to <u>re</u>gulate the heat in my <u>of</u>fice.

5. You<u>'re</u> different than my other Eng<u>lish</u> friends.

6. We<u>'ve</u> learned to expect better ser<u>vice</u> at the bank.

7. We<u>'re</u> sitting here waiting for the wait<u>ress</u> to pass by.

8. How can you just<u>ify</u> acting so infant<u>ile</u>?

9. What is the defin<u>ition</u> for <u>intra</u>-state?

10. The art<u>ist</u> was awarded the American<u>ism</u> award.

11. "The King<u>dom</u> of God is near," said the preacher.

12. I have one critic<u>ism</u>, that dress is too expens<u>ive</u>.

13. Deaf<u>ness</u> is a handicap that isolates man.

General practice with affixes, (continued)

14. Do you attend that fam<u>ous</u> <u>pre</u>-school?

15. Electric<u>ity</u> and water do not mix.

16. Yesterday I <u>re</u>newed an old friendship.

17. What is the oppo<u>site</u> of black?

18. Which is the worst handicap--blind<u>ness</u> or deaf<u>ness</u>?

19. Sure<u>ly</u> there must be something else that gives you plea<u>sure</u> besides reading.

20. In the pa<u>st</u>, it was not <u>un</u>usual to have a big party on the four<u>th</u> of Ju<u>ly</u>.

21. This is a pleas<u>ant</u> way to spend an evening that had been planned differ<u>ently</u>.

22. The marri<u>age</u> will take place in the ante-room rather than the hall.

23. Let us formul<u>ate</u> our plans for our "Employ<u>ee</u> of the Year" chicken dinner.

24. If you can <u>dis</u>engage yourselves for a few minutes, I have an announce<u>ment</u> to make.

25. That Chin<u>ese</u> teacher is very femin<u>ine</u>.

26. The insur<u>ance</u> company was doing something <u>il</u>legal, and the <u>fed</u>eral govern<u>ment</u> was about to <u>per</u>form an inspec<u>tion</u> of the company.

27. Our system of just<u>ice</u> is <u>im</u>perfect I am sure, but it is the best a<u>round</u>.

28. There are some bas<u>ic</u> rules one must obey when working with electric<u>ity</u>.

29. One must be able to just<u>ify</u> one's actions.

30. That femin<u>ist</u> has a devil<u>ish</u> look in her eye.

31. The drugg<u>ist</u> had an oper<u>ation</u> that was very expen<u>sive</u>.

General practice with affixes, (continued)

32. I want to empha<u>size</u> over and over again that
    deaf<u>ness</u> is a handicap even though it is not
    a vi<u>sual</u> one.

33. There are vari<u>ous</u> rules we should <u>re</u>-establish.

34. It is <u>un</u>necessary for me to say I am <u>pro</u>-
    Americ<u>an</u>.

35. The roar of the crowd was deaf<u>ening</u>.

36. Animals are lov<u>able</u>.

37. We have a short<u>age</u> of coffee.

38. His refus<u>al</u> to do the work cost him his job.

39. They fought for their free<u>dom</u>.

40. The toy was brok<u>en</u>.

41. It doesn't make any differ<u>ence</u>.

42. The stud<u>ent</u> studied hard.

43. The Bak<u>er</u> made cookies.

44. The wait<u>ress</u> served us well.

45. I want the larg<u>est</u> apple in the tree.

46. This is a joy<u>ful</u> holiday.

47. He went through bas<u>ic</u> training.

48. No one will not<u>ice</u>.

49. The lightning filled the air with elect<u>ricity</u>.

50. She is an <u>ir</u>responsible person.

51. The monkey is swing<u>ing</u> in his cage.

52. The baby has redd<u>ish</u> hair.

53. Are you act<u>ive</u> or passive?

General practice with affixes, (continued)

54. It's a hopel_ess_ cause.

55. They lived happ_ily_ ever after.

56. Your pay_ment_ will be $10.00.

57. The bright_ness_ of the sun is blinding me.

58. That operat_or_ gave me the wrong number.

59. It was a wond_rous_ time of year.

60. A _pro_noun takes the place of a noun.

61. His friend_ship_ was important to me.

62. She will speak _in_stead of me.

63. The comple_tion_ of the test was difficult.

64. No child is a fail_ure_.

65. The clouds moved up_ward_.

66. The circus had a funn_y_ clown.

67. There's a short_age_ of coffee in the cafeteria.

68. It's differ_ent_ when you like the person.

69. Those books _ante_date mine.

70. Are you _anti_-war?

71. The elector_ate_ will decide.

72. She _dis_likes too much work.

73. My king_dom_ for a horse!

74. I'll cloth_e_ you in gold and silver.

75. Her cheeks redd_en_ed fast.

76. All the employ_ees_ have to go.

77. He's interest_ed_ but not very interesting.

General practice with affixes, (continued)

78. The differ<u>ence</u> isn't important

79. She knows the govern<u>or</u> person<u>ally</u>.

80. Chin<u>ese</u> is Greek to me.

81. A lion<u>ess</u> can be fright<u>ening</u>.

82. You're the nic<u>est</u> guy I know!

83. This principle is bas<u>ic</u> to the whole theory.

84. Just<u>ice</u> is for everyone--we hope.

85. Can you just<u>ify</u> what you just said?

86. It's <u>im</u>possible to talk to you.

87. I hit the first percent<u>ile</u>. Aren't you proud?

88. He has a leon<u>ine</u> head of hair.

89. That idea is of <u>inter</u>national import<u>ance</u>.

90. He works for an <u>intra</u>state trucking company.

91. The comple<u>tion</u> of his studies is near.

92. You're being fool<u>ish</u>.

93. National<u>ism</u> may be good or bad.

94. She's s typ<u>ist</u>.

95. He always says exact<u>ly</u> the oppos<u>ite</u> of what he does.

96. The simpl<u>icity</u> of the idea is surprising.

97. Be creat<u>ive</u> in your teaching.

98. She special<u>izes</u> in modern art.

99. Slow<u>ly</u> but sure<u>ly</u> does it.

100. Don't sit under<u>neath</u> the table, please.

General practice with affixes, (continued)

101. Kindn<u>ess</u> pays off in the long run.

102. What a glori<u>ous</u> day!

103. The <u>pre</u>test didn't turn out very well.

104. A <u>pro</u>noun takes the place of a noun.

105. You'll have to <u>re</u>write that composit<u>ion</u>.

106. My <u>sub</u>conscious is trying to tell me something.

107. The tru<u>th</u> isn't always pleas<u>ant</u>.

108. Don't look so <u>un</u>happy.

109 I hate to move furnit<u>ure</u> around.

110. She's eas<u>y</u> to please.